W9-BMZ-184

*f*P

OTHER BOOKS BY MARVIN OLASKY

ON AMERICAN HISTORY

Fighting for Liberty and Virtue, *1995*
The American Leadership Tradition, *1999*

ON JOURNALISM

Prodigal Press, *1988*
Central Ideas in the Development of
American Journalism, *1991*
Telling the Truth, *1995*

ON POVERTY-FIGHTING

Freedom, Justice, and Hope (co-author), *1988*
The Tragedy of American Compassion, *1992*
Loving Your Neighbor (co-author), *1995*
Renewing American Compassion, *1996*

ON ABORTION

The Press and Abortion, *1988*
More Than Kindness (co-author), *1990*
Abortion Rites: A Social History of Abortion in America, *1992*

ON PHILANTHROPY AND PUBLIC RELATIONS

Corporate Public Relations, *1987*
Patterns of Corporate Philanthropy, *1987*
Philanthropically Correct, *1993*

ON RELIGION AND WORLDVIEWS

Turning Point (co-author), *1987*
Whirled Views (co-author), *1997*

COMPASSIONATE CONSERVATISM

What It Is, What It Does, and
How It Can Transform
America

♦

MARVIN OLASKY

THE FREE PRESS
New York London Toronto Sydney Singapore

THE FREE PRESS

A Division of Simon & Schuster Inc.
1230 Avenue of the Americas
New York, NY 10020

THE FREE PRESS and colophon are trademarks
of Simon & Schuster Inc.

Manufactured in the United States of America

10 9 8 7 6 5 4 3 2 1

Library of Congress Cataloging-in-Publication Data

Olasky, Marvin.N.
   Compassionate Conservatism: what it is, what it does, and
how it can transform America/Marvin Olasky.
      p. cm.
   1. Conservatism—United States. 2. Social ethics—United States.
3. United States—Politics and government—1993- 4.Decentral-
ization in government—United States. I. Title.
JC573.2.U6 O437 2000
320.52'0973—dc21

                                                          00-028284

                   ISBN 0-7432-0131-0

To the bold and courageous poverty-fighters
at faith-based organizations who are working
to transform America

ACKNOWLEDGMENTS

THE DISCERNING CRITIQUE of editor Bruce Nichols greatly improved this book. The wit, patience, and eye for specific detail of my son, Daniel, hugely improved our travel. The wisdom and compassion of my wife, Susan, enormously improves my life.

I am indebted to the Acton Institute for the Study of Religion and Liberty, which underwrote research and travel, and to leaders who guided me around their cities, including Kathy Dudley, Barbara Elliott, Bill Stanczykiewicz, Art Farnsley, Terry Cooper, Dean Trulear, and Leslie Gardner. My thanks also to the many social entrepreneurs and volunteers at faith-based organizations who answered my dumb questions.

CONTENTS

FOREWORD

by Governor George W. Bush

MARVIN OLASKY was the first to show brilliantly how our nation's history is one of compassion. Compassion demands personal help and accountability, yet when delivered by big government it came to mean something very different. We started to see ourselves as a compassionate country because government was spending large sums of money and building an immense bureaucracy to help the poor. In practice, we hurt the very people we meant to help.

Even now, some still look to big government, and others are content to let markets be our only guide. Marvin has emphasized a different view, and it is an approach I share. Prosperity is not enough. Conservatism must be the creed of hope. The creed that promotes social progress through individual change. The creed that mobilizes lessons of the past to produce effective reform. We are a wealthy country, but we have too many needy citizens. There are still too many for whom the American dream is distant. Compassionate conservatism is a conservatism that cares about them, and makes a concerted effort to help them bring lasting change into their lives.

Marvin is compassionate conservatism's leading thinker, and he has seen how lives change. He has personally helped less fortunate Americans. He helped to found New Start, a faith-based program that helps the poor spiritually and materially. He chaired a crisis pregnancy center. He and his wife adopted a needy child. He knows that when a life is broken, it can only be rebuilt by another caring, concerned human being.

Government can do certain things very well, but it cannot put hope in our hearts or a sense of purpose in our lives. That requires churches and synagogues and mosques and charities. A truly compassionate government is one that rallies these armies of compassion and provides an environment in which they can thrive. A government that knows its limits and helps people show what's in their hearts. A government that helps organizations of all faiths. A government that acts as a clearinghouse and catalyst for the natural compassion that is a hallmark of the American people. Government will not be replaced by charities, but it can welcome them as a partner.

This book clearly summarizes the principles of compassionate conservatism. But by showing how they have already been put into practice, in cities and regions spread far and wide, it offers more. Marvin offers not just a blueprint for government, but also an inspiring picture of the great resources of decency, caring, and commitment to one another that Americans share. He shows the difficulties that social entrepreneurs work to overcome, and ways for all of us to help them. Marvin's books provide vital insights for those who want to understand America's past and future. He knows that we can, as a society, do better than we did through programs developed in the 1960s. We can make the world more welcoming. We can share our resources—both material and spiritual—with those who need them most. Here's how.

CHAPTER ONE

A Brief History of
Compassionate Conservatism

COMPASSIONATE CONSERVATISM. Many reporters see it as a sugary concoction, word candy for a political campaign that seeks not to offend. But that conventional wisdom is wrong. Compassionate conservatism is neither an easy slogan nor one immune from vehement attack. It is a full-fledged program with a carefully considered philosophy. It will face in the twenty-first century not easy acceptance but dug-in opposition. It will have to cross a river of suspicion concerning the role of religion in American society. It will have to get past numerous ideological machine-gun nests. Only political courage will enable compassionate conservatism to carry the day and transform America.

That's the thesis of this book, which is being finished on Veterans Day 1999, one year after Texas governor George W.

Bush said on election night 1998 that he hoped to give the GOP a "compassionate conservative" face. Pundits pounded their laptops that evening, quoting a conservative governor's purportedly fluffy words, not understanding that he was working off a redefinition of compassion that had been a decade or more in the making.

Recovering a Dumbed-Down Word

The word *compassion* from the 1960s through the early 1990s was as much a code word for liberals as *family values* has become for conservatives. *Compassion* no longer conveyed what its literal dictionary definition states: com-passion as "suffering with," reflecting the close personal tie of a caring individual and a person in distress. Instead, hundreds of newspaper articles defined a compassionate legislator as one voting for a welfare spending bill. Those opposing such bills were cold-hearted and, by definition, uncaring.

In the early 1980s Bob Woodson, head of the National Center for Neighborhood Enterprise, challenged that apparent liberal monopoly on concern for the inner city. He argued that small neighborhood groups could do a much better job of revitalizing urban communities than could the grand projects of the Great Society. He put together conferences of street gang members gone straight and of tenants who wanted to manage and eventually own their housing projects. But Woodson did not yet have much of a constituency: liberals were still enamored with big government, and few conservatives paid attention to poverty issues.

In the late 1980s Howard Ahmanson, a Christian conservative from California, brought together poverty specialists and academic generalists to explore problems of Third World relief and development. The group found that poverty around the world is a spiritual as well as a material problem: most poor people don't have the faith that they and their situations can change. The group concluded that economic redistribution by itself cannot fight poverty effectively because it does not affect the attitudes that frequently undergird poverty.

I learned from listening to Bob Woodson and by participating in the deliberations of the Ahmanson group. In 1990 I wrote *The Tragedy of American Compassion,* which presented a history previously hidden in the stacks of the Library of Congress. The book showed how a century ago, before the federal government ever became involved, thousands of local, faith-based charitable agencies and churches around the country waged a war on poverty much more successful than our own. This history gave readers hope because they realized, as had American GIs in World War II, that "we did it before and we can do it again."

The historical record suggested that what worked a century ago to bring people out of poverty would still work, because social conditions were oddly parallel. Americans a century ago had problems with crime, alcoholism, and drugs (opium rather than crack cocaine). Rates of illegitimacy and divorce were far lower then, but more orphans roamed the streets because parents were sometimes carried away in epidemics. Faced with such difficulties, faith-based groups a century ago helped millions out of poverty and into homes. Local organizations had the detailed knowledge and flexibility necessary to administer the combination of loving compassion and rigorous discipline that was needed.

My Washington speeches and articles in 1989 and 1990 attempted to define what I was calling "conservative compassion." The goal was to break away from the equation of conservatism simply with a vote against welfare spending: "Conservative politicians have been complaining for years about a spendthrift modern welfare state—but they have been stating the problem backward. The major flaw of the modern welfare state is not that it is extravagant, but that it is too stingy. It gives the needy bread and tells them to be content with that alone. It gives the rest of us the opportunity to be stingy also, and to salve our consciences even as we scrimp on what many of the destitute need most—love, time, and a challenge to be 'little lower than the angels' rather than one thumb up from monkeys."

I hoped to see welfare transformed, as much as possible, from government monopoly to faith-based diversity. "The government of a pluralistic society is inherently incapable of tending to spiritual needs," I emphasized, "so the more effective provision of social services will ultimately depend on their return to private and especially to religious institutions." But *The Tragedy of American Compassion*, after being turned down by a major publisher, finally appeared in 1992 from a small house with a pea-sized marketing budget. The book fell into the giant puddle of words between overlooked covers and disappeared with hardly a ripple.

Mid-1990s Upheaval

Some people became aware of my book. One was George W. Bush, preparing to run for governor of Texas. In 1993 he and his key adviser, Karl Rove, got together with me to discuss the policy implications of my findings. At that time I knew of George W. Bush only as the owner of the Texas Rangers, and I looked forward to the opportunity to talk some baseball. In our discussion, though, he showed a keen and probing intelligence and an understanding of the history of poverty fighting. He asked questions that went to the heart of issues involving children born out of wedlock and men dying slowly from drug abuse on the streets. An excellent book published in 1993, Myron Magnet's *The Dream and the Nightmare,* also had had an impact on him.

In 1994 other leaders, among them former Secretary of Education Bill Bennett, John Fund of the *Wall Street Journal,* and philanthropist Heather Higgins, became aware of *The Tragedy of American Compassion* and started promoting its view of what was needed for serious welfare reform. That view began resonating politically in November as Republicans across the country astonished pundits by capturing Congress for the first time in forty years and thrusting forward Newt Gingrich. Meanwhile, George W. Bush surprised the Texas press almost as much by ousting a popular incumbent, Ann Richards. The two leaders in the spotlight had radically opposed styles. Newt in 1995 seemed always intense, while George W., though he would appear tough at times, was fully comfortable kicking back on the second-story porch of the governor's mansion in Austin, listening to Texas Rangers ball games on the radio, and looking at the brightly lit capitol dome.

Bill Bennett gave Newt a copy of my book at Christmas in 1994, and it moved the Speaker-to-be. Newt shocked me by repeatedly telling Republican congressmen, and everyone else throughout 1995, that they had to read *The Tragedy of American Compassion*. Newt's life became a tragedy in its own right; in 1996 he tried to reconcile with the press and moderate voters by projecting a friendly persona like that of George W. Bush, but his happy talk about beach volleyball appeared forced. In 1999 Newt made public some of the marital problems and extramarital activities that I believe contributed to his decreased effectiveness. Nevertheless, I still think of him as the bold leader of 1995 who made serious mistakes but pushed for real change that would benefit the poor, and not just more handing out of governmental spare change.

The Washington welfare reform debate of 1995 and 1996 was wild. I took a leave of absence from the University of Texas to spend big chunks of time on Capitol Hill. Senators John Ashcroft, Dan Coats, and Rick Santorum and Congressmen Steve Largent, J. C. Watts, and Jim Talent led the battle to obtain both welfare reform and congressional backing for faith-based community renewal. These leaders, who formed what eventually became known as the Renewal Alliance, moved past typical Republican sound bites about wasting dollars. They advanced the cause of compassionate conservatism by emphasizing the tragedy of wasted lives. We came up with some expressions that caught on: "effective compassion . . . challenging, personal, and spiritual help . . . warm-hearted but tough-minded" concern.

Half of our effort was successful. After President Clinton vetoed serious welfare reform bills twice, he signed one into law in August 1996 rather than risk a third strike as his reelection campaign was reaching a climax. The new legislation eliminated much of the negative, yet did little to accentuate the positive by, for example, offering help to organizations with strong track records in fighting alcoholism and drug addiction, or tutoring children, or motivating ex-convicts to avoid new trouble. The legislation pushed half of the welfare population to get off the rolls and (for most) to grab onto jobs over the next three years. But what about the faith-based groups that will help ex-welfarists hold those jobs as they build families and communities?

The Renewal Alliance offered alternatives to not only welfare but individual isolation. Its congressional members noted that people in trouble need a friend, a mentor, who is ready to help whenever a crisis occurs, but bureaucracies tend to operate 9 to 5. They explained that it's not the role of government to be the friend, but that those who govern must not block the mentor or clergy man from helping the person in need. They argued that government must not usurp the role of community and faith-based groups and must not set up barriers that frustrate those who wish to volunteer.

Nevertheless, the Renewal effort fizzled legislatively in Washington because of historical reasons (laid out in chapter 4) and current obstacles (examined in chapter 7). An opportunity arose for a farsighted governor to take the lead. George W. Bush was a natural, both because of his father's earlier interest in the "thousand points of light" and his own personal, faith-based change in 1986 from heavy drinking at times to abstinence from alcohol. It nevertheless took a particular incident to move him to an embrace of religious groups and the eventual decision to make compassionate conservative approaches the cornerstone of his campaign.

That incident came in 1995, the governor's first year in office. One state agency tried to shut down a Christian antidrug organization that was effective despite (or because of) its refusal to obey state requirements that counselors have extensive classroom training in conventional antiaddiction techniques. When three hundred of the group's drug-free alumni demonstrated with great Texas resonance at the Alamo, and *World,* the *Wall Street Journal,* and other publications covered the event, cards and letters poured into Governor Bush's office asking him to call off his regulatory dogs. He did, and then proposed (and in 1997 succeeded in having passed) legislation to pen them up permanently.

The governor did other things as well during the two years before his 1998 reelection campaign. He issued an executive order making Texas the first state to establish the option of using private and religious charities to deliver welfare services. He set up a level playing field for both religious and nonreligious groups for Texas social service contracts, abstinence education grants, and poverty-fighting initiatives. He made Texas the first state to permit a state prison unit to be operated by a ministry. He established alternative licensing procedures for many faith-based programs. He created a pilot program establishing Second Chance group homes for unwed teen welfare mothers run by faith-based and other private groups. He proposed and signed a Good Samaritan law that gives liability protection to health professionals who donate charitable care to needy Texans. He recommended and signed a law requiring governmental agencies to develop welfare-to-work partnerships with faith-based groups in a way that respects those groups' unique religious character.

Familiarity with Use and Abuse

None of those initiatives received much attention from the press, nor were they viewed as part of the major restructuring of government-societal-religious interaction that "compassionate conservatism" is beginning to connote. In part, the lack of press interest came from unfamiliarity with inner-city faith-based organizations. Most urban reporters know city hall and the way to crime scenes, while "charities" are often seen as fluff assignments for the staff sentimentalist. But in another sense, press cynicism about the term came from familiarity with the way the phrase had been used and abused for the past two decades.

Oddly, the first person to use the specific phrase *compassionate conservatism* during the past two decades, from what I've been able to uncover, was Vernon Jordan. In 1981 he attacked the Reagan administration for purportedly not showing it. He thus set the pattern for reporters who used or quoted the phrase as a liberal or moderate attack on conservatives.

Over the next fifteen years, various Republican politicians—most notably Orrin Hatch, Ray Shamie of Massachusetts, Bob Dole during his 1988 foray into presidential primaries, and Bob Dornan and Pete Wilson in California—spoke of conservative compassion, but none of them provided much in the way of specifics. Wilson muddied the waters by defining compassionate conservatism, according to the *Washington Post*, as a position that combines "old-fashioned budget-balancing with spending for preventive health measures and protection of the environment, and a strong pro-choice position on abortion." Biblical conservatives did not accept a mixing of compassion and abortion.

In the early 1990s, liberal reporters continued to equate compassionate conservatism with social liberalism. They were surprised during the mid-1990s when black conservatives such as Congressman J. C. Watts and magazine publisher Willie Richardson praised Newt Gingrich's Contract with America for embodying compassionate conservatism through its backing of a balanced budget amendment, tax cuts, welfare reform, and anticrime proposals. To include "getting tough on crime" in a list of compassionate measures showed a willingness to be tough-minded rather than mushy; compassionate conservatism, in this usage, was conservative. But Bob Dole muddied the waters again in 1996 by offering "compassionate conservatism, whatever" when he was accused of meanness. Journalists turned off by Dole's inability to articulate ideas, and running mate Jack Kemp's penchant for articulating all ideas in a continuous flow, tended to see the phrase as mere rhetoric.

Perhaps the first national identification of George W. Bush with the phrase came in an August 1997 CNN broadcast. Governor Bush, the reporter noted, had managed to gain "legislative approval for a series of tax, welfare and educational reforms he calls compassionate conservatism in the face of a Democrat-controlled state house." CNN offered no specifics, nor did other outlets. The term in its different uses was popping up occasionally. A Lexis-Nexis search shows that the phrase appeared an average of twice a year during the 1980s, but six times a year from 1991 through 1994 and thirty-seven times a year from 1995 through October 1998. Still, there was little meat on its bones.

As Governor Bush ran for reelection in 1998, he talked in a conservative manner about how some Americans had replaced responsibility for self with blame of others. He noted that Washington was only too happy to pick up responsibilities people sought to shed, and to erect massive, bureaucratic programs of material assistance, which eroded even further the civic institutions that had once linked assistance to moral accountability. He described how a minimizing of personal responsibility had pushed America toward a spiritual and moral crisis, with the familiar symptoms of broken or never-formed families, teen drug abuse and pregnancy, crime, civic disengagement, and disenchantment with public life. In short, he was laying out the history of our nation's long descent from true compassion to the liberal variety. Sadly, the press rarely picked up on his history telling, which ran counter to the conventional wisdom.

When election day 1998 was over, Newt Gingrich was heading toward retirement and George W. Bush was the front-runner for the Republican presidential nomination. The press reported that he received seven out of ten Texan votes but gave credit to a pleasant personality rather than his engagement with cultural decline and his desire to turn things around. Still, mention of the phrase *compassionate conservatism* exploded. The number of Lexis-Nexis stories containing that word zoomed to an annualized rate of 2,040 for the last two months of 1998, 3,164 for the first half of 1999, and 4,455 between July and October 1999.

Yet even then Governor Bush's message was interpreted for the American public not only by conventional reporting but by politicians operating within the box of conventional thinking. After the Bush "compassionate conservatism" victory remarks in November 1998, Vice President Al Gore said he thought people deserved more than "crumbs of compassion." Joe Andrews of the Democratic National Committee said, "Compassionate conservatism is a contrived copout." Harsh words came from Republican presidential candidates engaged in early jockeying. Former Tennessee governor Lamar Alexander called the term "weasel words"—clever but meaningless. Former vice president Dan Quayle ordered his staff "never—ever—to utter the words 'compassionate conservative.'"

Governor Bush's Stand

Those politicians and journalists did not know or understand the decade-long development of the concept and the fact that its conservative usage had iron in its spine. Bush did, and he did not back off. "On this ground I'll take my stand," he said. Then he counterattacked: "I know this approach has been criticized. But why? Is compassion beneath us? Is mercy below us? Should our party be led by someone who boasts of a hard heart?" He offered a general description of what his chosen label means: "It is conservative to cut taxes. It is compassionate to help people save and give and build." He continued the parallel structure: Conservative to reform welfare, compassionate to encourage charity. Conservative to set challenging educational standards, compassionate to make sure no child is left behind. Florida's newly elected governor, Jeb Bush, chimed in, "True compassion means suffering with the poor and acting on the consciousness of your suffering—and we should shift power away from the bureaucracy to the people in the compassionate community, who actually deal with these problems."

Governor George W. Bush did more than talk. He had begun to make compassionate conservatism more than a pretty phrase in Texas, but knew that much more needed to be done in the larger sphere. While much of the country lay freezing, Bush, on February 26, 1999, brought into Austin's warmth some of the best thinkers in the country to begin the process of developing more specifics. Bob Woodson came from Washington, James Q. Wilson from California, and John DiIulio from Princeton. Indianapolis mayor Steve Goldsmith invited others as well and chaired the three-hour meeting, but Bush was clearly in charge, pouncing on generalities and pushing for specifics, as he always does. By the end of the afternoon, major directions were clear and tasks assigned. (I was in charge of a religion and public policy task force designed to come up with concrete ways to aid the development of faith-based organizations.)

The process that began on February 26 culminated on July 22, when Bush spoke in Indianapolis. During the intervening five months, compassionate conservatism underwent further development in three stages. First, the ivy cabinet of policy conceptualizers came up with ideas and proposals. Second, Bush's kitchen cabinet of Austin advisers reviewed the proposals and tried to meld them. Third, Governor Bush decided which ones to run with and which to table. The goal was to come up with not only a speech but a set of specific initiatives, so that no one could reasonably say anymore that compassionate conservatism was a contentless phrase.

The speech that resulted clearly laid out a conservative philosophy diametrically opposed to the Washington-centralizing tendencies of recent decades. "In every instance where my administration sees a responsibility to help people," Governor Bush said, "we will look first to faith-based organizations, charities and community groups that have shown their ability to save and change lives." He took issue with the journalistic critiques and challenged pundits to see for themselves: "Sometimes the idea of compassion is dismissed as soft or sentimental. But those who believe this have not visited these programs. Compassion is not one of the easy virtues. At Teen Challenge—a national drug treatment program—one official says, 'We have a rule: If you don't work, you don't eat.' This is demanding love—at times, a severe mercy." He took on Al Gore: "Some Washington politicians call these efforts 'crumbs of compassion.' These aren't 'crumbs' to people whose lives are changed, they are the hope of renewal and salvation."

Governor Bush also proposed going far beyond conventional revenue sharing: "Resources should be devolved, not just to states, but to charities and neighborhood healers." He praised the work of religious groups and proposed a substantial change in the way government officials would deal with them: "We will never ask an organization to compromise its core values and spiritual mission to get the help it needs." He pledged specific institutional innovations: "We will set up a compassion capital fund, to identify good ideas transforming neighborhoods and lives and provide seed money to support them—helping to expand the scale of effective programs. . . . We will create an advocate position—reporting directly to the president—to ensure that charities are not secularized or slighted." He talked not only about ideas but gave a specific figure: $8 billion to provide charitable tax credits, expand the federal charitable deduction to taxpayers who do not itemize, provide other new tax incentives for giving, and support private and religious efforts that change lives.

After the speech, some journalists persisted in poking fun at such initiatives, as if the only programs of substance are those run by big government or big business. Those attitudes reminded me of my rookie reporting days at the *Boston Globe* in the early 1970s, when I was assigned to write a story about "the noodle priest." It turned out that a priest had developed a high-yield strain of grain that could make a difference in the lives of millions of people in Southeast Asia. That's not bad, but because he was working for a faith-based nonprofit operation, his story was part of the charity beat to which reporters with no clout were assigned. For some reporters in 1999, not much had changed. If a candidate did not know the name of a minor foreign leader, that was big news, but if he did know the names of some life-changing leaders in America's inner cities, that did not much matter.

Seven Principles of Compassionate Conservatism

Other journalists, however, particularly those from England, France, Australia, and other countries, were more curious. As I learned from July through October 1999, they often had two sets of questions. First, they wanted a list of principles that compassionate conservatives generally embraced. I was able to give them seven in ABCDEFG order.

Assertive

The preamble to the Constitution speaks of government promoting the general welfare but not providing it. Alexis de Tocqueville was astounded to see Americans forming associations to fight poverty and other social ills rather than waiting for government to act. Such assertiveness surprised Europeans well into the twentieth century. This quality is depicted well in one of my family's favorite movies, *The Great Escape*. In it, captured pilot Steve McQueen refuses to kiss up to the prison camp commandant, who asks, "Are all American officers as ill-mannered as you are?" McQueen breezily responds, "About 99 percent, yeh." Recently, however, many Americans have become better mannered, meekly paying taxes and expecting a paternalistic government to fight poverty. Compassionate conservatism is the opposite of a wimpy doctrine; it emphasizes a renewal of the citizen assertiveness that so impressed the first great foreign journalist to come here, de Tocqueville.

Basic

Compassionate conservatives choose the most basic means of bringing help to those who need it. The goal is to look within the family first; if the family cannot help, maybe an individual or group within the neighborhood can; if not, then organizations outside the neighborhood but within the community should be called on. If it is necessary to turn to government, compassionate conservatives typically look first to municipal, then to county, then to state, and only then to federal offices. At each governmental level, the basics should be in order before proceeding to the more complicated stages. For example, a group that protects teenage ex-hookers from pimps should have adequate police protection. Good Samaritan laws should be enacted so that a person who helps a mugging victim does not have to fear a lawsuit. When such basic protection is in place and counterproductive regulations have been replaced, the next goal is improve information flow concerning an organization and to facilitate contributions. Then it is time to bring in questions of direct grants, tax credits, and so forth, always looking to the most basic level of government that can act efficiently on a particular problem.

Challenging

The tendency of affluent Americans has been to turn poor people into pets, giving them food and an occasional pat on the head but not pushing them to be all they can be. Over time, bad charity has tended to drive out good, because people given a choice of pampering or needed pressure generally take the easy route. But those who consider the good of others as more important than their own satisfaction challenge clients (and themselves) to stretch self-perceived limits. Hard, character-building work is often particularly important in this process. Compassionate conservatives do not merely give the poor a safety net that may turn into a hammock; they provide a trampoline. The goal is to have the affluent stretch their limits also. It's easy to write a check but hard to check pride and arrogance at the door when dealing with those who don't get much respect, or to travel to a part of town that is outside the middle-class comfort zone.

Diverse

Since the 1960s, the vast majority of agencies to which those in trouble are supposed to turn have all had similar three-step approaches. First, *take a number.* The egalitarian goal is to ensure that everyone is treated exactly alike so that no one has any legal standing to complain. Second, *take your money.* Make sure that everyone entitled to benefits receives those benefits, even if the process enables people to stay in misery, instead of pushing them to become financially independent. Third, *take your religious beliefs outside.* God is supposedly banished from the premises. The compassionate conservative goal is to offer a choice of programs: Protestant, Catholic, Jewish, Islamic, Buddhist, atheist. Some programs may emphasize education, some family, some work. Compassionate conservatives make sure that no one is placed in a particular type of program against his will, but they also try to make sure that religious people are free to communicate their values.

Effective

While understanding the severe limitations of government poverty fighting, compassionate conservatives do not assume that all private philanthropy is good and all government programs are automatically bad. Some private charities can be as bureaucratic, unchallenging, and downright foolish as their governmental counterparts, so the goal is to ask tough questions. Does a program have a success rate that can be quantified? Is the amount a group spends per person sensible in relation to services offered and their outcome? Does a group mobilize community strengths by efficiently using volunteers? Does a program use the professional capabilities of those who volunteer? The two bottom lines of helping organizations— lives changed, funds used efficiently—need assessment. The quantity of people fed or bedded down is not as significant as the quality question: What happens to those human beings?

Faith Based

Judging by the historical record and contemporary testimony, well-managed, faith-based programs are more effective in fighting poverty, on the average, than their nonreligious counterparts. Research studies show that church attendance tracks closely with lower dropout rates, less drug use, and fewer crimes committed. Faith-based organizations have shown that the best way to teach self-esteem and respect for law is to teach that we are esteemed by a wonderful God who set out for us rules of conduct that benefit society and ourselves. For civil rights reasons also, the First Amendment's guarantee of freedom *for* religion should not be taken to mean freedom *from* religion. Therefore, for both pragmatic and philosophical reasons, compassionate conservatives insist that the Bible (or the Koran) should not be excluded by judicial fiat from any antipoverty work, including that financed by government, as long as individuals have a choice of programs.

Gradual

The pragmatism of compassionate conservative suggests careful checking on what works and what does not, each step of the way. A typical process (to use a Texas example) would be to start with one faith-based prison program, check results, and then expand it if graduates of that program have a reduced rate of recidivism. Similarly, to see if tax credits will increase the resources of nongovernmental antipoverty groups in a way that benefits society, the plan is to start with a limited program and then expand it if the pluses outweigh the minuses. The goal throughout is gradual, sustainable change, tested at each step of the way, rather than a revolution that could be quickly followed by counterrevolution.

Evaluation from the Ground Up

That's the big picture I tried to paint for journalists and guests from abroad. But they also asked about the street-level reality, and here I told them about what I had seen during June and

July 1999. During the weeks before Governor Bush gave his Indianapolis speech in late July, one of my sons and I traveled to seven big cities, with a particular mission in mind.

Here's the background. When *The Tragedy of American Compassion* drew national attention in 1995, I took my third-oldest son, Daniel, then ten years old, to Washington for a round of Capitol Hill meetings. He also sat through talk show interviews and collected souvenir M&Ms at the White House. We went together to speeches I gave in a few cities, and he became a conference connoisseur: the best had bottles of soda in the back and bowls of candy at the tables. It was all great fun for a ten-year-old.

In 1999 Daniel turned fourteen, and by then he had thoroughly absorbed my riffs. I could ask him, "What's the literal meaning of compassion?" He would answer, "Suffering with." I could ask him, "What's wrong with just giving money to a homeless guy?" He'd reply, "It's not challenging him to change."

It was endearing to have a son who knew my work, but it was also a bit disconcerting. I wondered, might Daniel know too much about compassion in the abstract and not enough of the reality? If Daniel equated welfare reform to Washington souvenirs tucked away in his bedroom, was that good enough? I decided that Daniel should meet the people behind the statistics. Maybe he would not only come to understand compassionate conservatism in a far deeper way, but would also see that investing in lives is often better than investing a bit more in 401Ks. So on June 1, 1999, Daniel and I hit the road, on our way to visiting antipoverty programs in Texas, the Midwest, and the East.

By the time Governor Bush gave his speech and more journalists started calling me, our travels were done. The travel had changed Daniel in several vital ways, but had also changed me. I became convinced that the best way to understand compassionate conservatism is not to go through a list of theoretical statements but to walk the streets of our large cities and talk with those whose faith is so strong that they refuse to give up. I also became convinced that the best way for me to present the real problems and opportunities is to show what Daniel and I saw and heard—and not in a neat, wrapped-up form but by giving a sense of the variety that we saw. Chapters 2, 3, 5, and 6 do just that. Chapter 4 is a break that presents some important historical background (for Daniel and I talked history a lot as we traveled), and Chapter 7 sums up.

CHAPTER TWO

TEXAS

Land of Social Entrepreneurs

O N JUNE 1, 1999, Daniel and I left Austin and headed north on the interstate that connects Dallas to the Mexican border but also connects Texans to some notorious history. We drove through Round Rock, now an Austin suburb but in 1878 the site of one of Texas's most famous shootouts. Texas Rangers were waiting on July 19 when stagecoach and train robber Sam Bass decided to diversify into banks. They wounded him severely. He died two days later and was buried in the old Round Rock cemetery, located on what is now Sam Bass Road.

Ten miles later we hit Georgetown on the San Gabriel River, the starting point of many cattle drives after the Civil War. Next came Salado, a stop on the Old Chisholm Trail, with a Stagecoach Inn whose guests included George Armstrong Custer and Jesse James. We zipped through Belton, once known to travelers as a good whiskey stop, and on to Waco, a town so wild after the Civil War that stagecoach drivers asked passengers to strap on their guns as they approached "Six-Shooter Junction."

As we drove we listened to some tunes by Robert Earl Keen, a poet of the new Texas. His ballads recount broken dreams and broken families: "You got in some trouble in high school. But you feel like a new man today. You keep to yourself, cause anyone else, would just as soon blow you away." We listened to another Keen song of defeat: "If I could live my life all over, it wouldn't matter anyway. Cause I never could stay sober, on Corpus Christi Bay."

Home-grown Dallas Leaders

South Dallas, the first stop on our tour, could be a setting for a Robert Earl Keen song. The heat on June 1 was already radiating as we drove down rundown blocks that were almost urban clichés with their storefront churches as well as George's Liquors and Super Discount Package. Dilapidated wood-frame houses, smaller and shabbier than double-wide mobile homes, were the backdrop for people clutching forty-four-ounce bottles of malt liquor.

But hidden behind the city's crumbling facade live some modern Texas heroes willing to take on today's bandits. Calvin and Johnnie Mae Carter, for example, are a retired couple who now run a community center in their rundown but optimisti-

cally named neighborhood, Sunny Acres. The Carters early in
the 1990s wrote 150 letters to the Dallas chief of police about
drug and crime problems, describing how drug dealers
blocked off Sunny Acres streets so they could sell dope more
easily. Police response was slow, in part because of concern that
arresting black drug dealers would open them up to accusa-
tions of racism. The Carters pledged their support for police
action, and other black leaders joined them. Finally the police
arrived and rousted the dealers.

The Carters set up a community center in a former crack
house that they bought for $2,500. The general equivalency
diploma (GED) classes and tutoring they offer now give a second chance to young men caught in the drug industry. "Once
people are trained, once they're computer-literate, the jobs are
there," Carter answered, rubbing his hand through salt-and-
pepper hair. "But it takes a lot to turn around a twenty-one-
year-old who can't read." "That's right," Mrs. Carter chimed
in as she offered some cookies. "We need to teach those young
parents who let their kids do whatever." Those young parents
rarely had kind but tough parents of their own, but now they
do: the Carters.

Daniel really liked these grandparents who exuded both
determination to change their neighborhood and a sense of
contentment at what they have been called to do, win or lose:
"God's in charge," they say. Unpaid and uninstructed, the
Carters had developed a welfare program that works—a local,
unsupervised, tailored effort by highly dedicated people. And
the question immediately comes to mind: Can more couples
like the Carters come forward? How can they be helped?

The Carters are not alone. We visited Reverend Stephan Broden, who runs the Fair Park Friendship Center and its summer education and evangelism program for forty elementary school-age children. His resident teacher, Tim Oostdyk, is so excited by the program that he delayed poking himself with his insulin shot in order to tell Daniel and me about the end-of-summer trip to Colorado for the sixteen or so children who would prove themselves conscientious. Curriculum is cleverly tied to the trip. Students learn math by computing travel distances, geology by studying mountains, and history by hearing about the development of the West. They study Bible passages concerning mountains, eagles, and hawks. To go on the trip, kids have to earn points for achievement in tutoring sessions, so they have a big incentive to keep coming all summer.

The center is obviously a poor place, with well-used furniture and fourteen old, donated computers (some very old, with big floppy disks). Still, most are good enough to run programs such as Math Blaster and Jump Start. Each student brings in fifteen dollars for the cost of the Colorado trip, and the Friendship Center provides a 90 percent subsidy of the actual costs. The church-funded group is providing a public service by giving youngsters who could otherwise afford nothing but trouble a productive way to spend their time, so it would make sense for the public to be involved.

And yet Broden has heard so many stories of heavy-handed government funding that he said he would not accept even a basketful of bucks: "There is no way we could take that money, although we desperately need it. We might as well shut down." He was convinced that government funding would mean an end to teaching about Jesus, and "the reason we're here is that kids need to come to Christ." I asked, "What if some government funds without those strings attached would allow you to expand your program?" He said that he lacked sufficient faith to believe in such a possibility (and he's right, in recent history). So the Fair Park Friendship Center limps along, doing wonderful but limited service, as thousands of children roam the streets.

In Dallas's southern and poorer half, Daniel and I met Jackie Mixon, founder of the optimistically-named Ideal Neighborhood Association. She's a no-nonsense, forty-four-year-old former schoolteacher who brought up her three children in a house her grandfather had built. But the house could not hold back time, decline, and drug dealers who started bossing the neighborhood. Mixon started asking neighbors who owned houses not to rent them to dealers, but the dopers made threats, and most people gave in. She recalled, "Some of the neighbors were afraid to even come out on the porch. We had these yards with weeds as tall as a person. The drug dealers hid stuff there and threatened to blow us up if we talked."

Finally, one elderly woman refused to rent out part of her duplex to dealers. One day, as she was talking on the telephone, dealers invaded her home and threw her to the floor. When she screamed, neighbors came to her aid. Then they held prayer walks, cooked dinners to raise money to set up a neighborhood association, and sponsored neighborhood cleanups. Mixon emerged as the leader and had to spend several nights in motels as dealers threatened her life. Finally, the police responded: "Undercover cops came in. In six weeks, the drug dealers were gone."

"So do you trust government now?" Daniel asked. Mixon laughed and replied, "Government men always wanted to do things their way, even if neighborhood folks had a better idea. Different government agencies come over and they all say they'll put money in, but they become discouraged and then they leave." She started chuckling so hard that she had trouble catching her breath. "They'd rather go to an easier neighborhood, I suppose," she finally said. Mixon's neighborhood is no longer a hell for the elderly, but it's not much closer to the ideal.

It seemed that wherever we went, leaders were springing up and working hard, but often with a sense of isolation and a lack of resources, not to mention a hostility toward government. The Ideal Neighborhood now had a neighborhood association, but vacant lots remained, drug dealers came back, and youngsters were still going to bad schools and dropping out. Welfare reform in 1996 could have increased the ability of experienced neighborhood leaders to help their communities, but instead they were often asked to produce bricks without straw. They found themselves running little enterprises without the necessary training or material.

Three unconventional Dallas leaders, seeing the problems, have tried to help.

A Gymnast Gunslinger

Kathy Dudley is by appearance more a gymnast than an urban gunslinger, but by sweet doggedness she's a bit of both, agile yet ready to duel. For close to a decade I've known Dudley, who is now forty-four and maintaining one of the best smiles west of the Mississippi. She spent fifteen years helping to revitalize a poor West Dallas neighborhood, and in 1995 set up the Dallas Leadership Foundation to bring similar change to other parts of the city.

Dudley uses her persuasiveness and her network of friends to bring resources into the poorest parts of Dallas, but everything is mediated through her memories of growing up poor in Appalachia. She still speaks of standing in line for a Christmas doll to be given her by some organization. After waiting a long time in the cold, with people across the street watching and laughing, she received one that was "naked and dirty. I looked at it and thought, 'This looks just like me.'"

Sympathetically trying to avoid such negative lessons, she has worked over the past several years with twenty-eight church and business groups to set up a store where some six hundred poor families could obtain Christmas presents at about one-fourth of the retail price. Parents make the selection. Parents, not the government or a nonprofit government look-alike, give toys to their children. Similarly, when she learned that residents of the Owenwood Neighborhood wanted yard lamps, she worked with a company to have 125 yard lamps installed, with residents paying about 10 percent of the cost and donors underwriting the rest.

Dudley is able to mobilize a thousand volunteers each year from rich and poor neighborhoods to rebuild and paint Owenwood homes, clean up and landscape streets and yards, and paint over graffiti. Last year, five construction companies and their subcontractors donated materials used to renovate five homes owned by elderly residents who had given years of volunteer community service. The neighborhood association chose the beneficiaries. Among them were Olan Turner and his paraplegic son, Erik, who had his neck broken in a football accident. Turner, a community bulwark for years, was gratified to see their home receive $50,000 worth of renovation. He now puts in ten to fifteen hours each week volunteering for community maintenance and development.

Compassionate people get involved in direct charity work like this. Compassionate conservatives attempt to bring governmental resources to bear on such efforts in a way to encourage rather than nationalize them. Much of the basic work is to have government offer the same measure of protection of people and property that it provides in affluent neighborhoods. That's hard going when for years criminals have been ceded effective control of some streets, but the rule of law is fundamental to community revival and the building of enterprises and habits of work. The government projects she has seen, Dudley said, thoughtlessly tout "visible stuff" over "people stuff." Officials, she said, work above ground rather than "building trust and developing roots." They always want to pass out money to build housing, she added, but her goal is the building of families and communities: "We're not interested in just doing housing."

Dudley and I have talked enough so that I know she's not a conservative, yet she talks like a conservative whenever the topic of government help is raised. She has taught me that poor communities need leaders like the Carters who stand up for neighborhoods they've lived in for years—but government officials, in her experience, cannot stand someone else being the leader. They "will support particular services," she said, "but government has to take the lead and it wants a monopoly on the overall plan." Instead of promoting community leadership development, such intervention undercuts whatever may be arising. The Dallas Leadership Foundation, on the other hand, does not have an accidental name; the emphasis on leadership means differentiating heroes from hustlers and stressing equipping and empowering rather than redistribution.

Dudley's concern about government action is convincing, particularly because she is not a multigenerational conservative viscerally opposed to seeing government folks as helpers. She was the youngest of twelve children, three of whom died young. Her dad was a poor sharecropper who became disabled when she was five and turned to despair and alcohol. Her life as a teenager was emotionally difficult, but she emerged with a faith in Christ and a college diploma, made possible by government-provided scholarships. Then she wed and lived in the Dallas suburbs, occasionally selling Tupperware and working as a fitness trainer. That lifestyle changed in 1982 when she, along with her husband and two small children, moved to the poor West Dallas neighborhood so she could dive back into a pool similar to the one from which she had emerged, barely breathing.

Social entrepreneurs cannot frighten easily. When Dudley wanted to start a program in West Dallas, she walked down a street with a soccer ball and a Bible, telling kids she wanted to play soccer and read them Bible stories afterward. They came.

She moved from a swank suburban home to an inner-city duplex. When someone threatened by her arrival loosened the lugs on the back left wheel of her van so that the wheel would come off while she was driving (mercifully, it fell off when she paused at a stop sign), she stayed the course. But government scares her. Early in the 1990s one official offered her a $170,000 grant, but she asked, "If I take this money and hire a housing director, I will hire a Christian and expect a certain standard of behavior. If the director has sex outside of marriage, I will fire him immediately. Do you have a problem with this?" Yes, the official told her. She spurned the grant.

Since Dudley believes in fighting both spiritual and economic poverty, she is bothered by proffered government grants that force her to choose between those two emphases. "Evangelism is central to everything we do," she muses. "Our mission is discipleship, so if the government gives money to gain one result of the mission, housing, but at the same time tells us to give up the mission, that makes no sense." She also tells of Owenwood neighborhood residents who received government money but had to use government contractors who did the work improperly and ended up doing so much damage that others had to be hired to repair the mess.

Yet Dudley has a yearning to do more, and she knows that more resources are needed. She is thinking through ways to avoid a governmental embrace. One of her main goals is to reinvolve members of the black middle class with the poor from their own race. She is a member of St. Luke's Community Church, conveniently located on the Interstate 30 access road so members can zip in and out without having to remember the neighborhood in which they grew up. She sits on the purple-padded pews in the stained-glass sanctuary and thinks of ways to bring the fifteen hundred commuter worshippers back to the poor blocks near the church that many once called home. She hears sermons asking members of St. Luke's, now a political powerhouse, to vote and show up at city council meetings. And she wonders how her church can become a center of person-to-person compassion.

As she waits for St. Luke's to come alive, she emphasizes the basics with folks from some of those storefront churches that fight liquor stores for strategic corners. The basics—weeds, paint, graffiti, outdoor lights—show whether a community is on the way up or the way down. While those at Housing and Urban Development in Washington dream of big projects, the struggling poor themselves often know far better what makes a difference. When Dudley was trying to help organize a Hispanic neighborhood, four people showed up at her first meeting, and one woman purportedly did not understand English. But when the subject of yard lamps came up, that woman started speaking in English, and she brought her friends to the next meeting. Twenty people showed up, and the privately funded effort with a tangible, vital product—street lights—took off from there, without red tape tangling good intentions.

One way to multiply the efforts of private charity is to bring big and small churches together—and bring together poor and rich churches as well. Along with working at St. Luke's, Dudley is bringing together some South Dallas neighborhood churches with rich ones, such as Highland Park and

Park Cities Presbyterian Church to the north. Sometimes, though, it's hard to teach both sides that alliances of that sort cannot be based primarily on money. Private funding is no guarantee of success. Partners need to develop mutual respect, with an emphasis on decision making by those who have to live daily with the results of the decision.

Sometimes it seems easier for a camel to go through the eye of a needle than for the rich to listen to the hard-working poor. Government, sadly, has developed the habits of the rich. "It's possible to work out a collaborative relationship with a government group," Dudley mused, seeing it almost as an unrealistic hypothetical: "Maybe we'd train a family in responsible home ownership, and then the city could kick in money to make housing affordable. But that means a church group is making the decision, and the government goes along with that decision. Do you think that's really going to happen?"

An Optimistic Realist

That history of government failure to allow religious liberty also occupies sixty-one-year-old Ben Beltzer, head of Interfaith Housing Coalition in Dallas, and a legendary poverty fighter whom I wanted Daniel to meet. When Beltzer talks about his experience with government, negatives pour out: "Too much red tape. You have to be very careful not to mention the word 'Christ.' I once applied to FEMA [Federal Emergency Management Agency] back when we started in 1985, and a big check came pretty quickly. But the check came in a box that was filled with lots of stuff—manuals, instructions, warnings, and all that. I said, 'uh-uh, I'm not doing that.' I boxed up all the stuff with the check and sent it all back. They said, 'You've accepted it, you can't send it back.' I said, 'I've done it.'"

Gruff Ben Beltzer is no fan of government, yet he is also skeptical about typical volunteer do-goodism, maybe because some people sweet on the outside soured his life for a time. In 1974 he was a credit manager for Borg-Warner with an entrepreneurial hankering, so he gave up his steady job to enter the tire business alongside a man he trusted. That man cheated him, he says, and at age thirty-six, with four children, Beltzer was unemployed for fifteen months. "I felt the same pain, the same fear," he says, that some of the people he's now helping feel. "How did you get out of it?" Daniel asked, and Beltzer looked him in the eye and said, "Five men held me accountable. They never allowed me to wallow. Accountability. Responsibility. That was crucial."

What Beltzer has built on his own since then, with the help of individual and church contributions, is a program that champions responsibility as the way out for a hundred women and their children each year. He and they work and live in old buildings on or near Ross Avenue on the eastern side of Dallas. Ross begins at Dallas's historic west end, with its re-creation of the first cabin built there and its X marking the spot where John F. Kennedy was shot. The avenue then pushes glamorously past modern and postmodern skyscrapers, including the Trammel Crow building with its collection of Asian art. But Interfaith Housing is east of that, in a poor neighborhood. One interior wall of the office displays writing from children who live in Interfaith's temporary housing and have basic needs: "I thank God for letting me still be here on EARTH." "I thank God for letting me live." "I thank God for a place to live." "I thank God for helping me in situations where times were rough."

Sadly, many children who could give thanks there do not, as the sins of irresponsible parents are visited upon them. Potential clients for Interfaith receive referrals from shelters, churches, and government agencies. Almost all who call are scheduled for interviews, but only half of those who call show up. Of those who show up, only half enter the program. Those who test positive for drugs or alcohol or show no interest in working are not allowed in. Once in the program, each woman receives a plain, comfortably furnished suite for herself and her children in an Interfaith building, but she needs to work. She begins her morning with a motivational Bible lesson. She then sits in a cubicle calling places that are hiring. She has to travel to interviews; Interfaith provides haircuts, professional clothing, and bus fare. Crucially, Interfaith also provides day care for children under five years old, an after-school program for older children, and assurance that those who snag jobs will not be left in the lurch concerning medical and dental needs.

That no-excuses emphasis on employment, not just work-delaying job training, is one key to the program's success. Almost every woman finds a job within three weeks. It doesn't matter if her skill levels are poor, Beltzer says in his no-non-sense way: "Most of the women have milked the government out of data entry courses, which means they usually can't do it, but places will train them." It doesn't matter if women have criminal backgrounds or bad credit reports: "I tell them, just tell me the truth and tell the employer the truth. Be matter of fact: 'I screwed up then, but things are different now.'" In Dallas's strong economy, jobs are readily available, so it's not hard for a woman during her thirteen weeks in the program to save $1,200 to $1,500, which is enough for a first month/last month rent payment.

A second key to success is the emphasis on responsibility that runs through the program. "We never tell them what they can't do," Beltzer insists. "We do tell them the steps they need to take, and we have goal evaluations every thirty days." When Daniel asked about the residents who do not meet the goals, Beltzer minced no words: "Remember, these poor people are survivors. They're experts at milking the church. They love Christian do-gooders. But we hold them accountable to their dream." Residents are held accountable regarding the budgets they have constructed: "They bring in receipts for every penny they spend, so we can show them the difference between shopping at the 7–11 and going to the supermarket. It's not that they don't know the difference in prices between the two, but they don't know how small differences add up."

Strict rules are the third key. Women may not have male visitors. Those suspected of drug use are tested, and anyone who tests positive is out. Staffers make random checks, and anyone who tests positive is out. Residents are required to work hard to get a job and work hard to keep on working. Anyone who skips out of the job search process on two days is out. "I don't feel guilty," Beltzer says. "They've chosen to leave. We tell them, 'When you're here, you'll make choices, and those choices will determine your future.'"

The fourth key is to avoid either pandering to or abusing volunteers. Beltzer is sarcastic about "holiday season soldiers": "Sure, Thanksgiving and Christmas, the only time the poor are hungry. We'll sometimes have a request from a Sunday school class that wants to adopt a family for December 21–28. The class wants to see the kids say, 'Thank you, thank you.'" Beltzer will not put up with such selfish altruism. He asks volunteers to make at least a one-year commitment. In return, Beltzer pledges in a brochure for prospective volunteers that their time will not be wasted with bad-attitude clients: "Only those who are committed to making life changes that lead to long-term stability are admitted into the program. The Interfaith staff interviews and screens candidates before acceptance."

With those ground rules established, about 250 volunteers each year—most from churches, some from the Junior League—come forward so that each of the twenty-five families in residence each quarter receives ten co-partners. A host family prepares the first meal for a moving-in mother and children and makes sure that they have a week's supply of groceries. The hosts do no counseling but serve as friends—people to whom the residents can explode when the pressures seem overwhelming. Each resident family also has two employment and two budgeting co-partners who help with résumés and discuss interviewing and financial successes and failures. The two co-partners may take on good cop–bad cop roles. Other volunteers help out with children or teach about nutrition, menu planning, and comparison shopping. They offer counsel about holding onto a job, communicating with children's teachers, and becoming a better mother. They often pray with residents and offer Bible studies.

The depth of co-partnering gives both residents and volunteers options when personalities clash. Beltzer is also careful not to throw in volunteers over their heads. For example, staff professionals rather than volunteers counsel children, almost all of whom have been abused psychologically and often physically. Volunteers are pampered not by making their work easy but by identifying their gifts, building community for them, and caring for them: "If a volunteer is in the hospital, we'll be there." A few of the volunteers eventually become underpaid staffers. Sherri Ansley, for example, worked for a division of PepsiCo that designated Interfaith Housing as its charity and wanted to keep working there as an accountant, but "God tugged at my heart for four years." For the last two years, she has been an Interfaith Housing staff member.

Daniel was impressed with Beltzer's tough-minded approach, honed over two decades of poverty-fighting experience. The numbers Beltzer provided also looked good. Since Interfaith's inception in 1985, seven of every ten women entering the program have successfully completed it, with two-thirds of those becoming financially independent over the long term, according to Beltzer's estimates.

After visiting neighborhood leaders like the Carters and then savvy social entrepreneurs like Dudley and Beltzer, Daniel was thinking that a new war on poverty would be easily winnable, so I was glad when Beltzer pointed out that a program like his can't change people who aren't ready to change. And then Daniel and I did the math. Half of those referred (50 percent) show up for interviews, and half of those (cumulatively, 25 percent) enter the program. Seven of ten complete the program (cumulatively, 18 percent). Two-thirds of those make it. So overall, 12 percent of those who could be helped by the program actually are. "That's right," Beltzer said. "Tell the truth: Life is tough." It is. Some governmental programs over the years tried to do a Beltzer-light (setting up rules and not always abiding by them), but they often found it hard (and sometimes politically impossible) to hang even semitough. Tossing people out of a program feeds into one major criticism of compassionate conservatism: that it is simply a shifty means of shredding the safety net. If enough people fall through, it is easy to claim success with the rest.

Real help for the rest, however, will come not by lowering standards but by challenging all who are able to aim higher. If government programs no longer enable people who could do better to maintain their bad habits, then more will show up for the interviews Beltzer offers, and more will come ready to work instead of failing drug and drinking tests. Then the challenge will be to expand Interfaith Housing to serve more people without dumbing down the program—and perhaps government officials will learn to send checks in envelopes rather than in big boxes packed solid with red tape.

Putting Together the Pieces?

The third major Dallas catalyst I wanted Daniel to meet was Don Williams, fifty-seven, who five years ago restructured his job as CEO of Trammall Crow Company, the nation's largest real estate developer, so he could devote half his time helping to bring poor Dallas neighborhoods back to life. We met him in his office on the top floor of his company's building, and Daniel was impressed with the whole ambiance. He told me, "Great view. Other people who work here are wearing coats and ties, but he doesn't. He calls out softly for a folder, and his secretary knows exactly where to find it."

It wasn't always that way for Williams, who grew up in New Mexico, didn't go to a prestigious college or law school, and began practicing law in Dallas in 1966. He joined Trammell Crow Co. seven years later and in 1977 became the company's chief executive officer and managing partner. He worked very hard and earned a hefty salary. He also stayed married and had five children. But in 1994 he gave up his day-to-day responsibilities and became Trammell Crow chairman so he could spend half his time on the Southern Sector Initiative, designed to help Dallas's southern (and poorer) half. It was time to move from success to significance, he says; after building a business, it was time to try building a community.

I explained to Daniel that this is not only a remarkable story but, if history points to the future, a failure waiting to happen. Williams may be only the latest in the line of those who believe that downtown visions can make a difference on inner-city ground covered over by social kudzu. From Great Society efforts in the 1960s through recent efforts like the Atlanta Project, a Jimmy Carter attempt to transform his city, successful businessmen and politicians had hired urban planners, looked out from skyscrapers at pedestrians scraping the ground, and failed conspicuously. But it's also possible that Williams will break through, because he has studied the failures of the big projects and can identify reasons why: "Atlanta Project, $3 million in overhead. Sandtown [Baltimore:] became a service provider instead of a catalyst, and administrators said, 'We're gonna do this, then this,' instead of listening." Others, like a glitzy Rebuild LA project that followed the Rodney King riots, emphasized above-ground building rather than the Dudley approach of sending down roots and learning to distinguish heroes from hustlers. Williams said, "It's taken four years to get to know the people."

The big positive for Don Williams's program is the people he's getting to know: those who emphasize faith-based solutions. Unlike the secularists who dominated the big projects of the past and selected neighborhood recipients made in their image, Williams looks for "gamebreakers," those who can revitalize a depressed team, and believes that "gamebreakers are without exception people of faith." His organization for scouting and then supporting gamebreakers is the Foundation for Community Empowerment, which has four full-time staff members and an $800,000 budget supplied largely by Williams himself. The FCE sees church initiatives as leading to "the spiritual, moral, physical, psychological, and economic health of neighborhoods." Crucially, "spiritual" comes first.

Williams's methodology follows from his emphasis on faith-based organizations. The community institutions that stand out in neighborhoods are churches and liquor stores. Fighting devastation contributed to by the latter, after it already has happened, is Sisyphus-style catch-up. It is far better, Williams notes, to accentuate the positive by helping to develop the faith-based assets that neighborhoods abundantly have. In 1995 Williams and an assistant, Candace Gray, set up meetings with pastors, principals of two religious academies, and some public school principals as well. The three questions Williams asked are ones useful in any antipoverty effort: What are your critical needs and your crucial assets? What are you doing to effect change? How can we be useful to you?

It will take several more years before we know whether Williams's FCE is a resounding success, but his departure from previous efforts is striking. As Daniel and I drove away from Dallas, we knew that new efforts to effect encouraging change were underway, but wondered whether they were enough to counter the negative influences—poor schooling, the lure of drugs and crime, and inadequate teaching in some churches— that were driving poor communities down.

The Networked Houston Haves

Daniel and I thought about Don Williams's three questions and ours as we drove over to Houston. The nonprofits we visited over four days there were easily divisible into the haves and the have-nots. The crucial divide occurred not over vision but over the ability to network with the affluent and gain relatively risk-free donations. Some of the haves were doing a good job and deserved their funding, but many of the have-notes were at least equally deserving, yet were isolated—sometimes because the program heads were overtly ardent in their faith and determined to press ahead their way.

We started by visiting an organization that has on an entryway plaque the unambiguous goal that characterized its founding nearly a century ago: "Star of Hope Mission, Dedicated to the Glory of God." Long-term clients are housed in a two-year-old building that is clean, carpeted, and spacious, with residents housed in individual rooms and family suites with doors that lock. They proceed through a structured program that has three phases: Career Development, Personal Development, and New Hope, a ninety-day substance abuse program. Clients typically work half the day and take life skills, spiritual development, and GED courses during the other half.

The new building is Star of Hope's Transitional Living Center. With the two other buildings, one for men and one for women and children, Star of Hope can shelter close to four hundred persons; in the course of a year, it houses over four thousand individuals and serves half a million meals. Those are big (and costly) numbers, but Star of Hope's financial success is evident. Outside every room is a plaque showing which individual or organization paid $6,000 to furnish it. A computer learning center is one of several inviting common rooms. Those who stay for ten months receive a bonus of two thousand dollars that can typically be used for the first and last month's rent and other housing expenses on the outside. Organizations that helped with the building's $12 million cost included Conoco, Exxon, La Quinta, Shell, and NationsBank—and the federal Department of Housing and Urban Development.

Here is a well-connected mission. Has some price beyond cash been paid for the excellent facilities? Star of Hope, despite its entry plaque, seems to deemphasize its Christian origin and minimize the centrality of conversion in radically changing lives. Some volunteers might like to proselytize, but Star of Hope discourages one-to-one interaction of volunteers and residents. Daniel, a bit of a romantic, thought Star of Hope seemed cold, antiseptic, a bit like a government look-alike. That's probably unfair, because this shelter was a lot better than those in the smelly, crowded, and unsafe buildings that are typical in many cities—but both of us were uneasy.

Daniel and I visited another one of the "haves" to see how government can help to reinvent education. KIPP ("knowledge is power program") Academy is a charter school that receives government funding but has some freedom from the education bureaucracy. Its 275 middle school students arrive at 7:25 A.M. and leave at 5 P.M. on weekdays. They also attend school on Saturday morning and for one month during the summer, knifing through Houston heat and their own desire for vacation.

The students, 95 percent of them Hispanic or black, live by the motto on KIPP's walls: "There are no shortcuts." They are not students destined for success before they enter KIPP in the fifth grade. They are from neighborhoods filled with illiteracy, drug abuse, broken homes, gangs, teenage pregnancy, and juvenile crime. Almost all are poor, qualifying for the federal free breakfast and lunch program. Almost half in the fourth grade failed the TAAS test a basic skills exam required in all Texas public schools.

When these students enter a culture that emphasizes learning and hard work, their world changes. Fifth graders in one of the classes we visited were chanting, "Gotta read, baby, read!

Gotta read, baby, read," and "Knowledge is power, power is money, I want some." They have learned that education is their ticket out of poverty. Without a moment's hesitation, they can state the year they are planning to enter college.

Students sign a "Commitment to Excellence" form pledging diligence in attendance and homework. Parents agree to look over homework and push their children. Teachers sign the form also, pledging to be at the school during the extra hours and to be available for evening consultations by phone. The quantity of hours by itself does not do the job; more hours at many schools would be wasted. KIPP teachers are passionate about teaching, and they relish the opportunity to move beyond standard practice.

The change from the culture of barely getting by to a culture of excellence makes all the difference. A seventh-grade math class we sat in on was studying the same material as Daniel's eighth-grade class at a good Austin school. Students in an eighth-grade English class were discussing a poem not by giving their "feelings" about it, but by analyzing carefully its meter and metaphors.

Hard work at KIPP is paying off; the school's TAAS test results over the past three years have made it a state leader. The Texas Education Agency has recognized KIPP as a TEA Exemplary School each year since 1996. The *Houston Post* honored it as 1997's Best Charter School. Daniel came, saw, and was conquered. "The desire to learn is so apparent in these students," he said as we headed out. "What a great place!"

The recognition KIPP received has been important for both morale and money. Contributions and foundation funding have made possible extra teacher pay for those extra hours and class trips that persevering students receive as a reward. For example, fifth-grade students study government and take a field trip to Washington, D.C. (On one recent trip, KIPP teachers induced Justice Stephen Breyer to talk to the students. He uttered a few pleasantries and then recognized a student who was vigorously waving his hand. The student proceeded to ask the justice how he had voted in *Miranda v. Arizona*. A surprised and amused Breyer said that case was before his time, but then dived into much more substantive comments.)

Despite encouragement and inducements, a few KIPP students are unwilling to trade immediate gratification for long-term satisfaction, they leave rather than stick with the hard work. Those who do study pass the basic skills tests and keep going. Most will be prepared for successful careers at leading universities, and they won't need racial preferences to gain admission. KIPP is a modern manifestation of what Booker T. Washington taught a century ago: attaining a life of achievement and freedom means getting up early, staying up late, and using the time in between for intense effort.

Daniel and I talked about this, and we agreed that those who think they are being kind by asking for less than 100 percent are actually doing harm by sapping the sense of urgency that is the mother of determination. And yet one element missing at KIPP was the one that Booker T. Washington emphasized. As his daughter Portia wrote, "We never at home began the day without prayer, and we closed the day with prayer in the evening. He read the Bible to us each day at breakfast and prayed; that was never missed. Really he prayed all the time." Washington emphasized that biblical understanding "must be woven into the warp and woof of our everyday life." A teacher's praise motivates good students for a time, he noted, but when the going gets rough, students need an internal gyroscope.

Washington stated that the vital religious sensibility might not show its importance every day, but it would always make a difference in the clutch. Those given the chance to cut corners without being caught needed the internal pressure to "live honored and useful lives, modeled after our perfect leader, Christ." Those given the opportunity to get rich quickly but unethically needed the sensibility to say no. Washington said, "A student should not be satisfied with himself until he has grown to the point where, when simply sweeping a room, he can go into the corners and crevices and remove the hidden trash which, although it should be left, would not be seen."

Excellent though KIPP is, it is a public school, and its students miss out on that added dimension.

Houston Have-Nots

Star of Hope and KIPP were networked with financial backers, though in different ways. Some conventional teachers and administrators dislike KIPP; its success makes it harder for them to justify their own failure by saying that poor youngsters from single-parent homes are unteachable. Nevertheless, the success of KIPP's students is irrefutable, and the school's future seems assured. But we also visited some high-achieving organizations that are virtual orphans, and we wondered what would happen to them.

Take, for example, Inner City Youth, a sports, Bible study, and education program in Houston's rough Third Ward. The organization is run by Prince Cousinard, a former professional baseball player whose home is now a refuge for kids abandoned by drug-dealing dads. Only five of the five-hundred kids whom Cousinard has helped in the last half-dozen years had an ongoing relationship with their father. They had no experience with a father who showed love by, among other things, laying down the law.

Cousinard gains initial respect by competing on the basketball court, the place "where manhood is taught in the ghetto. It's my pulpit. I can't let myself be run off." His year-round program—baseball, basketball, football, cheerleading, leadership training, speech and drama, academic improvement, and backpacking—draws kids off the street and instructs them in moral conduct. Cousinard and his wife, Sheila, become the parents that kids are essentially without, and the kids in turn so frequently make Cousinard's house their own that his door handles are worn out and his plumbing breaks down from overuse.

Cousinard is vividly aware of the alternative. He pointed out where a five-year-old boy in his daughter's class died at a nearby apartment complex. The boy was ripped apart by five bullets from a 9-mm automatic pulled out after his mother got into a fight with her boyfriend. "As I stood at the casket looking down at this little kid, it just broke me," Cousinard recalled. "He used to come to the fence here when I would drive by saying, 'Mr. Cousinard, can I play ball for you?' I have to wonder what would have happened if I could have had him with me that day instead."

Toughness and compassion go together in Cousinard's life. If he does not throw an elbow on the court, he won't have a chance to bring wary kids to a freshly painted church building, which, unlike its suburban counterparts, boasts beds for the desperate and a row of curtained showers. But Cousinard's approach does not work nearly as well in the corporate boardroom as on the court. His long-term plan comprises lots of handwritten notes. His budget would not get past a cautious bean counter. His vision of helping abandoned kids is clear from the work he does, but ask him to present it and a stream of disjointed sentences, with abundant but unorganized Bible references, pours out. Financially, Cousinard is struggling.

We also visited Youth-Reach Houston, a Texas-licensed group home–ranch east of the city. It was opened by Curt Williams, forty, who wears his long black hair pulled back in a pony tail. Addictions to drugs and smut—"My brother had a photographic memory and I had a pornographic memory"—ruled Williams's life from 1979 through 1984. Like most other addicts, he set up lines he said he would not cross: "I'll do drugs but I won't sell them. Then, I'll sell them but I won't sell them to kids." Finally, Williams crossed that last line and with "Critter," his best buddy, lived a life of misery and paranoia. Williams's only real friend was his mother, who would ask him how he was. When he said, "Fine," his mother would reply, "'I'll see what I can do about that.' She would pray that I be miserable," because only then would a decision to change come.

In 1984 Williams followed a pretty girl into a church and found welcome there. He kept visiting, although he repaid the kindness of church members with insults and continued drug use, until "one day I was so fried I couldn't tell time or tie my shoes." Having hit bottom, he went to church and felt spiritually compelled to throw away his drugs and pornography. He bought a Bible and study guides. He consumed them. His theology changed, and his life followed.

Williams then founded Youth-Reach Houston and tried to give kids what they needed most: someone paying attention to and challenging them. "Most of these kids had no dads and received no discipline," he said. "Kids who have grown up lazy need practice doing chores." Rules, penalties, and a willingness to expel kids to the streets are vital to the program. Behavior results in reward points, with residents allowed to advance through three levels. To teens who make no progress, Williams insists, "Change your attitude or change your address." He is only about five feet, six inches tall but has big muscles (Daniel whispered, to me, "He'd get my attention").

Counselors also show compassion, in the literal meaning of "suffering with." One dreaded punishment is picking up logs from a huge pile and moving them 250 feet into the field, for no purpose except discipline. Kids get angry but are impressed to find a staff member coming alongside them and lifting as well. That sometimes destroys the anger. Other work also teaches lessons. Each boy learns responsibility from being assigned a horse. (City kids have to learn to approach the horse from the side so as not to be bitten or kicked. They first avoid stepping on dry horse turds, but are soon throwing them at each other during a break.) Joint projects, such as rebuilding boats, teach cooperation. Bible study and worship teach underlying purpose.

The program works and could be expanded, but financial resources are limited. Currently, twelve churches and many individual contributors supply Youth-Reach's $250,000 annual budget, and staff members, including the Williamses, work long hours, receiving room and board plus two-hundred-dollars per month. But any likelihood of expansion is low as long as Williams and his wife, Shelley, announce, as they do in their newsletter, "We are unapologetically a Christ-based program." Material transformation is not Youth-Reach's chief object: "Our top goal is not to meet the physical needs of the poor or oppressed,"the Williamses write. "Our philosophy is that for a man to die with a full stomach and enter hell is a great waste and a moral tragedy. For a child to have new clothes and keep an old heart is an example of misdirected energies."

Funders have not flocked to such a program, even though it works. Nor do many people outside inner-city areas know of Houston's Mission of Yahweh, which provides literacy and computer training for poor women, many dumped by their boyfriends. Mission of Yahweh occupies several crowded wooden structures that contribute to the no-nonsense, boot-camp sense. Clients also must sign a zero-tolerance policy regarding drugs: "Any resident and/or employee of the Mission of Yahweh caught engaging in theft, drug or alcohol related activities, dishonest behavior, or other activities unbecoming to God and this organization will be promptly dismissed from the premises."

Victory Fellowship is another little-known resource. This religion and rehabilitation site for those who have been homeless or addicted has an opposite look from Star of Hope. The sight of folks crowded together in a dilapidated building might move foundation funders to pity, but checkbooks are rarely opened for something that doesn't look respectable. The books are balanced only because they don't exist. The only long-range strategic plan is to pray constantly—and yet, faithfulness does not mean that budgets are unnecessary.

Daniel and I saw other organizations that are effective but could not receive help from government and many private funders for two reasons. First, these groups proselytize. Counselors think clients need God and say so directly. Potential funders who not agree with that but are still moved by the results have to decide whether to put up with proselytizing in order to fight poverty. Second, the groups need to proceed in a businesslike way. Potential corporate or foundation founders are accountable for the grants they make and need an accounting from their grantees. Besides, some semiformal planning and organizing will not only impress potential corporate or foundation funders but will improve the efficiency of the groups themselves.

Individual and Governmental Roles

One sign of hope for the future of such groups in Houston is the recent appearance of an organization, the Center for

Renewal, designed to connect small, proselytizing, neighborhood groups with well-heeled, cosmopolitan funders. Every city needs someone like Barbara Elliott, the center's head; she can step over the broken glass outside homes like Cousinard's but also schmooze at fancy galas. She has led corporate funders on tours of the inner city and talked the language of business, emphasizing the need for "results-driven, cost-effective, and innovative" nonprofits. The Center for Renewal website is a useful resource for foundations, churches, business, and individuals who want to contribute to groups or learn about effective organizations and their best practices.

Maybe that's what groups need: passing around of information, and networking of the sort that Kathy Dudley and others provide in Dallas. Daniel and I were not sure such a procedure would enable the good groups to grow and replicate as rapidly as they were needed, but it wasn't as dangerous as entering into a duet with government. We started thinking that compassionate conservatism, government-style, should perhaps be restricted to buildings owned and run by the government, such as prisons.

The last stop on our Houston trip was a look inside one of the prisons to check out InnerChange, a program based in neither the conservative lock-'em-up-bury-the-key approach, nor the liberal rehabilitation-but-leave-out-God idea. The tell-tale indication that we were approaching the Jester II unit located southwest of Houston was that the roadside signs changed from come-ons for model homes: "Texana plantation estate homesites" to "Do not pick up hitchhikers." Then we walked in, behind prison walls topped with razor wire, and saw the new, "InnerChange" approach being developed by Prison Fellowship.

The plan is easy to define: a Bible-based, eighteen-month, prerelease program that emphasizes how God can change hearts. The outward changes are easy to see: 150 prisoners in white cotton shirts and trousers live in cubicles rather than cell blocks, but only a little thievery occurs. Inmates spend their nonwork hours in classes and Bible studies rather than in front of a television. Civil tones rather than profanity dominate conversations in front of visitors but also, according to prison officials, almost all the time.

Texas Governor George W. Bush gave the program a try, and state officials kept the American Civil Liberties Union (ACLU) at bay by giving all organizations, religious or atheistic, the opportunity to propose values-based prerelease programs. Several non-Christian groups inquired, but only Prison Fellowship went all the way. The state undergoes no expense, since Prison Fellowship supplies the staff and picks up other costs as well. Prisoners from any religion are allowed to join (and a couple of Muslims have), so there is no discrimination for or against any religious group.

The keys to success, according to Prison Fellowship, are God's grace and man's mentoring. Some prisoners reenter "the free world" with good intentions but quickly fall into old ways. (Sometimes a prisoner's father brings him back into the family dope business.) But as Governor Bush puts it, InnerChange "encourages people to stay involved with prisoners, changing one life at a time." A Christian volunteer assigned to each prisoner meets with him one night each week at the prison for two to three hours, helps him find a job and a church home following release, and does six months of post-prison mentoring.

The average InnerChange participant has had three prison terms. Donnie Gilmore, for instance, was pushing thirty with a résumé of breaking into houses and stealing cars—"doing anything I thought I could get away with," he said. Gilmore's interest in the program was piqued after his four-year-old daughter asked him about Jesus, and he realized he had never opened a Bible. Another participant, Donald Osage, had reflected on his former heroin addiction and the crimes he committed to support his $300-a-day habit. He realized he had to change his thinking or else he'd quickly shoot up again following his release.

Currently, 60 percent of released inmates nationwide return to prison. Near the end of 1999, with the program only two years old, InnerChange's rate was 17 percent, but some of the ninety-five program graduates had not been out long, and most states measure recidivism after three years. Both Gilmore and Osage talked about their conversion to Christ and how much they had learned through the fourteen hours a day of work, Bible study, classes, prayer, discussions, and community service that make up the program. Would that be enough to keep them and their peers from falling back into old patterns once they were no longer regimented? Many liberals prefer psychological approaches, and many secular conservatives scoff at such hope, but to those with faith in God-directed movement, InnerChange is a reasonable risk. Near the end of 1999, Iowa and Kansas were establishing larger versions of the Texas model, and several other states were contemplating the same.

What had Daniel and I learned about compassionate conservatism by the time we finished the Texas part of our travels? Faith-based groups were growing, slowly. Some initiatives were impressive. Small groups relied on government for fighting crime and running off drug dealers. Beyond that, the general advice that faith-based organizations offered concerning government resembled that of George Washington's concerning U.S. relations with foreign countries: "Avoid entangling alliances."

Networking, we had seen, was essential, but maybe individual and private networkers could find ways to do the job. Could and should faith-based organizations get any help from government, either in overcoming barriers to their work or in developing reliable funding? We didn't think so, but we were off to Indianapolis, the city of Mayor Steve Goldsmith, chief domestic policy adviser to Governor Bush's presidential campaign.

CHAPTER THREE

INDIANAPOLIS
How Government Should Work

T O SOME JOURNALISTS, compassionate conservatism sounds like "reinventing government," the new paradigm of the early 1990s, because both ideas emphasize local decision making, flexibility, and competition. That's true, and reporters who see "reinventing" as hype should be skeptical about compassionate conservatism, but they should also take seriously the dimension of faith—more potent than a drive for efficiency—that this new paradigm brings to the table. From what I had heard, Indianapolis would be a good place to see whether the attempt to reinvigorate faith-based organizations could bring civil society back to the inner city, but I was also skeptical, for I've been disappointed with claims about philanthropic wonders many times before.

Daniel and I drove into Indianapolis, a flat city with straight streets and a square look that was developed early in the nineteenth century. Some residents who moved in with the state government in 1825 were encouraged when the National Road (now U.S. 40) burst across the plains in 1834. They expected an industrial boom—sawmills, paper mills, factories!—when the Central Canal was built on the White River in 1836, but industry departed when the White River's muddy shores proved too fluid to maintain the canal. Only in 1847, with the coming of the railroad, which prized dull, level ground, did the man-made environment become just as workable as one that naturally had easy river transport and inexpensive water power.

Indianapolis's lack of natural advantages did make for one setback early in the twentieth century when it battled to become the center of the new automobile industry. City leaders gained an upper hand in marketing when on Memorial Day 1911 they inaugurated the Indianapolis 500, which has become the most-attended annual single-day sporting event in the world. But it was easier to get steel and coal into, and vehicles out of, Detroit, by the Great Lakes. Indianapolis remained a grain and livestock center, and its growth in the second half of this century came via not only man-made products but high-tech ones: first Eli Lilly and Co., the pharmaceutical king, and then automation, robotics, and computer software companies.

Daniel and I tried to get the lay of the land of a city without landmarks. As we drove up Meridian Street, the north-south avenue that divides the city's hemispheres, the economic stratification resembled a saga of twentieth-century American economic history. Old duplexes with splotchy paint between 30th and 38th Streets seemed to belong in a Depression. North of 50th Street and onward into the 60s, however, affluence emerged. Elegant residences and massive stone church edifices dominated this promised land that seemed to stretch all the way past 90th Street and into a new millennium.

The View from the 25th Floor

When we rode the elevator to what is known in Indianapolis as "the 25th floor," the top one at city hall, we saw the panorama from above. Mayor Steve Goldsmith gazed out from the large windows of his conference room and told us of concentric circles emanating from downtown. He pointed below to a small circle of gentrification. He gestured out farther to a drop-off-the-table descent into poverty. He extended his arm almost parallel with the floor to indicate a middle-class circle farther out and affluent homes on the horizons. Some 850,000 human beings in all live in Indianapolis, and 1.2 million in the metropolitan area, with most trying to find their proper distance from the urban bulls-eye.

Goldsmith then turned our attention from the horizontal to the vertical, not only the view of the ground from the 25th floor but the relationship between belief in God and hope for man. "Only hardened skeptics have trouble accepting that widespread belief in a Supreme Being improves the strength and health of our communities," he said. "Government can accomplish more by working with faith-based groups than it can ever achieve by circumventing them." Goldsmith is a thin man of average height who would fare well against urban tough guys only if they were coming out of a Bible study. Still, since he is Jewish, it was surprising to learn that the crux of his mindset was the importance of the cross: "In many of our most troubled neighborhoods, the most important asset is the church."

Goldsmith showed irritation as he described how past government officials have been not only reluctant to work with those assets, but hostile. He described his initial experience in spending some federal summer job money through faith-based organizations that reached out to neighborhood youngsters. When a state regulator complained that he had violated the terms of the agreement, Goldsmith expressed surprise, for that summer the money had actually been used for kids rather than stolen. But the regulator complained that "you allowed the young men and women in the program to participate in a voluntary prayer before lunch."

Goldsmith's major initiative as mayor stressed how the 25th floor can help those on the ground come together in action. He built what is called the Front Porch Alliance, a civic switchboard that during the 1990s worked with faith-based and other civic organizations to develop eight hundred partnerships for neighborhood action. Staffers left the 25th floor to knock on the doors of churches and small businesses. They set out to learn how to help neutralize the government bureaucracies that have often kept leaders from doing basic things to improve their neighborhoods.

This jujitsu use of government to beat government led to some "pretty basic" successes, Goldsmith says: "Churches get titles to crack houses down the street. Twenty or so churches have small contracts to maintain neighborhood parks. They meet the children and often involve them in their programs." The goal, he stressed, is "enough government participation to be supportive, not enough to distort." The key is identifying and working with the numerous "part-time pastors committed to transforming their blocks. When they had problems with bureaucracy, our goal was to make sure those problems were solved. The roadblocks became our problem, not theirs. We thought that they should not have to shop the bureaucracy."

Goldsmith had also paid attention to the negatives (high taxes, red tape, bad schools) that drive middle-class people away from the city. Realistically pessimistic about the reinvention of public schools in his city, Goldsmith (like Rudy Giuliani in New York) has been using his bully pulpit to promote Catholic schools. He has succeeded on the tax front by emphasizing competition in service provision; here he is like those government reinventors who put up a real fight instead of switching back to mega-government approaches. Contracting out microfilm services saved nearly $1 million over three years; window washing, $45,000 over the same period; printing and copying, $2.8 million over seven years. Competition to service the city's swimming pools and utilities saved nearly $500,000 over seven years. The city saved $15 million to $20 million on trash collection over three years. So it went, area by area, with every function except police and fire put out for bid. Total savings: $400 million.

Some city functions were privatized (since when are municipal employees the best managers of golf courses?), but

Goldsmith emphasized that his goal was competition, not necessarily privatization. He encouraged government employees to compete for contracts as long as they could do a quality job for a lower cost than others. Tax-saving stories emerged. The street repair department had thirty-six middle managers supervising ninety crew members. Faced with having to put in a competitive bid, union members recommended sending out four workers and one truck to fix problems rather than two trucks with up to eight workers, including a supervisor. Those requests were granted, and the union won the contract by cutting overall costs more than 25 percent without reducing service levels.

Creating more efficient government is important, but Daniel and I also wanted to know if government, which in recent decades has often hindered the work of religious groups, could this time provide help. Yes, Goldsmith insisted, as long as officials partnered with rather than patronized potential allies. Outsiders heading into inner cities could err by arrogantly assuming that they knew best, or by simply handing out money to those who styled themselves as heroes but were actually hustlers. The key to success was commitment to spend time listening and then work hard doing. A Front Porch Alliance, Goldsmith said, will work "anywhere there are committed people."

That was his view—but how did that work out at street level, in the areas where (according to the stereotypes) commitment was hardest to find? Just as denizens of the different circles tend to view their nonneighbors stereotypically, so "the 25th floor" sounds like a phrase that, coming from an inner-city resident, would be less like a term of endearment than one to be used scornfully and followed by spitting on the sidewalk. It was time to leave the mayor's marble-patterned, cherry-trim conference table and head into what Goldsmith had called the "drop-off-the-table" circle of poverty.

Cutting Through Bureaucracy

Daniel and I left the 25th floor and drove to Shepherd Community Center in what is called the near east side. ("Near" means near downtown geographically, although the area's poverty leaves it psychologically distant.) We talked there with Reverend Jay Height, executive director of the center (which includes a Nazarene church), and Bill Stanczykiewicz (pronounced STAN-juh-KEV-ich), who set up the Front Porch Alliance while he was a Goldsmith aide. They make an odd pair. Height is a chubby, soft-spoken man who was wearing khakis and a C.O.P.S.—Christians Obediently Preaching Salvation—shirt, while Stanczykiewicz has the tall, blond, and blazered good looks of a TV sportscaster, which is what he used to be.

The two worked together when Height became possessed by the idea of closing down an alley near his church that had become an ideal location for drug dealers and prostitutes. That alley emptied into another that offered three escape routes. Conveniently located pay phones at the McDonald's on one side of the alley and the Speedway gas station on the other supplemented the dealers' cell phones. This drug site by a main street, offering both visibility and invisibility as desired, was busy. During one mission meeting, Height recalled, "we watched five deals go down. Drug dealers are businessmen. They go by the real estate credo: location, location, location." Daniel, wondering whether closing one drug marketplace would make a difference, asked, "Can't they sell on any main street?" Height cited a study showing that 93 percent of street corners are not appropriate for dealing. Drug sellers need visibility to be seen, but not too much, and they need multiple escape routes.

What was needed to close down the alley? First, community organization. Ironically, the alley was just off what had once been the National Road, Indianapolis's great hope in 1834 for overcoming the city's lack of natural advantages. The street had since become part of the national drug road, but local business folks, helped by a Front Porch Alliance staffer who made phone calls and went door to door passing out fliers to get church and civic groups involved, formed the Old National Road Business Coalition. Jay Height became its president. The phone lines between his new civic switchboard and city hall began lighting up, illuminating another great barrier to action: numerous governmental agencies had some voice in the future of an alley off the road that had been a nation's pride.

A second step was to cut through red tape. Closing the alley took approval from fifty-one government agencies and private groups. Stanczykiewicz says simply, "We went through the red tape and got the alley closed." Height went further, comparing politicians who just talk with those who walk: "FPA walked the whole process through." The previous week Daniel and I had heard Joni Mitchell's song about those who "paved paradise and put up a parking lot." But in this situation, the reverse happened: Public Works department workers jackhammered an alley, chopping up and hauling away the concrete.

The third step would be a slow dance in most cities: destruction is easier than construction. But in Indianapolis, volunteers from Youth for Christ and Keep Indianapolis Beautiful quickly lay down trucked-in topsoil, shrubs, mulch, and twenty nursery-raised pear trees. In August 1998, the park that had been an alley opened, at a cost of $900 of donated funds. A plaque notes that the space is officially in honor of Indianapolis patrolman Matt J. Faber, who was shot dead on August 14, 1988, while investigating a complaint nearby. Faber's widow and mother attended the park dedication.

"When we work together, we can turn the tide," Height proclaimed. "This is our neighborhood. It's not the crack dealers' neighborhood." The Indianapolis Police Department backs up that statement. Drug sales are gone from the area, for there were no "good" drug business locations nearby. The alley closure created momentum for more progress. Police set up bicycle patrols, rousted prostitutes in the area, and ran stings to nab male customers. A larger park in the neighborhood that had been a haven for illicit sex is clean enough for kids and families again. Crime is down 10 percent in the area. When neighborhood leaders complained that a local bar was accepting food stamps for alcohol, with hungry children often left at home, police and other agencies worked to have the owner charged with welfare fraud. The state Alcoholic Beverage Commission ordered the bar closed.

Height is pushing on. He asked the Front Porch Alliance to help him obtain a small piece of land owned by the power company in back of his church: "Steve Goldsmith called the company's CEO and asked him to donate the property. He said yes, and now we're putting in two playgrounds. The FPA held my hand, took me through the process, filled out the paperwork—a huge task—and helped me through two hearings." Height also had a fence put in, much to the consternation of one criminal, who was running from the police and ran right into the unexpected barrier. "He was dazed," Height smiles, but Height also has been dazed by the support he has received in trying to take dominion over one little patch of Indianapolis: "The FPA knows city hall. I don't, and I don't have the time or ability to figure it out. I know the near east side, my neighborhood, and the Bible. So I'm impressed that the FPA has opened doors and taught us the procedures."

Height's Shepherd Community Center, in addition to a church, has a nonprofit charitable organization, the Shepherd Community Development Corporation (CDC). Shepherd CDC has worked on developing job opportunities that meet needs of local businesses; current components include Shepherd Lawn Care, Shepherd Mailing, and Potter House Pottery, designed to mold clay and souls. Much of Shepherd's effort focuses on children, with after-school sessions and a summer program for which mothers pay seven dollars to enroll a child for the entire summer. ("I've learned," Height says. "When the program was free, 50 percent of the kids wouldn't come. Now that I charge a little, 90 percent come.") But his church is a small one, with Sunday attendance of about one hundred, and expanding the program will require outside funding.

Where to get it? In Indianapolis Steve Goldsmith made limited government funding available to help with church-run programs that benefit children in impoverished neighborhoods, as long as private funding takes care of specific worship and prayer functions. But Height is nervous: "We're not going to dance around to get funding. We'll say, 'Here's who we are, here's what we do.'" He also wonders about bureaucratic tie-ups: "Bill Stanczykiewicz is great, and Steve Goldsmith can love what we do, but an operator thirty levels below him can hold things up. And it can take a long time to get money. I don't have six months' money in savings."

Height's message gave us pause. Compassionate conservatism, we were seeing once again, is hard to put into practice. A river of suspicion runs through Dallas, Houston, and Indianapolis, and religious leaders and secularists see it as too deep to ford. Maybe the most that can be done is helping to get rid of problems that faith-based organizations face, like a drug alley across the street. But what about using taxpayer funds to expand good programs that could reach many more?

All Kinds of Ingredients in the Stew

Going further will require a huge degree of give and take from both sides. It was easy for Daniel and me to like the seemingly tireless Jay Height. We admired his devotion to his church and his refusal to give in to drug dealers. We both had a different reaction to a central northeast-side minister, the Reverend Ann

Henning-Byfield, but we learned something in the process about the pluralism inherent in compassionate conservatism.

We met Henning-Byfield in the old fire station that the city had turned over to her church, Robinson Community AME (African Methodist Episcopal), to become Village House, a neighborhood center. A big, brassy woman, she was wearing a yellow print dress and sitting in an office with sports equipment, including a croquet set, pushing out from the corner. She quickly told us that she did not like "ultraconservatism" and made it clear that she was giving us time only because we were allies of Goldsmith, who was also ultraconservative in her opinion but nevertheless "empowered some people who were not The Leaders. He listened. He found a way to meet people who were out here doing something."

So Daniel and I listened as Henning-Byfield described herself: a Democrat who embraces "womanist, Afro-centric liberation theology." She described Goldsmith as "a shrewd man. Here's a mayor known to be Jewish openly embracing Christians. That's very smart." She sees herself as a pioneer, overcoming opposition within her denomination to female ordination and accumulating along the way a notable series of firsts: the first woman invited to preach to the Indiana AME Annual Conference, the first woman delegate from Indiana to the AME General Conference, and the first black woman president of the Indiana Interreligious Commission on Human Equality. Her preordination work with the U.S. Department of Labor, where she managed equal opportunity programs, helped to prepare her to defeat opponents she views as reactionary.

Henning-Byfield is not to the taste of most conservatives, but neither is her neighborhood a place savory to most tastes, except those addicted to danger or depravity. It is one of the top ten syphilis sites in the United States, with lots of "commercial sex workers" plying their trade. She says, "The health department told me, 'We don't care what you do. You can pray, you can teach, but stop the rash of syphilis.'" So she teaches that the wages of sin are sores and proposes faithfulness to one partner as an alternative. Since spring break is a big initiation time for gangs, Village House has all kinds of activities that week as an alternative. Since latchkey kids get into trouble, Village House emphasizes after-school care, but she knows that is not enough: "We have them for two hours a day, but often the mother's crazy and the stepfather's on drugs."

Although she is suspicious of Goldsmith, she gives him credit for surprising her. The Front Porch Alliance, she says, gave her "access to people in the city without my having to find out everything myself. The mayor put all these people out front and said, 'These are your servants. If there is a drug house in your neighborhood, here's who you go to. If you have a problem with code, here's who you go to.' He's supported ministries for years without ever asking the ministers to speak for the mayor or show up at political functions." (I later asked around about this and learned something extraordinary in urban politics: No one was ever asked, let alone coerced, to plant a yard sign or make a political speech on behalf of Goldsmith as "payment" for help from the Front Porch Alliance.)

Village House received some small grants from the city for utility expenses, but Goldsmith "also taught us about private resources that could be available. I asked Eli Lilly for $150,000 for a spiritually based, nonsectarian program, and I received $220,000." Daniel asked whether Henning-Byfield felt strange working as a pastor while running a nonsectarian program. "Schizophrenic," she replied. "If I'm not careful, talking with some white official at 9 A.M and at 11 A.M. counseling a momma whose son is in jail, I cross the line." But what is the line? Summer camp includes no Bible teaching, but Henning-Byfield, like Ralph Reed, knows the value of a mailing list. "I've got their names and addresses," she says of her campers, so "when I do vacation Bible school, I'll send an invitation to kids in summer camp. And look at our Bible posters." Daniel and I did, walking next to the wall as children peeked shyly from their chairs: "Queen of Sheba, Powerful Ruler." "Pharaoh's Daughter, Caregiver to Moses." "Ethiopian Eunuch, 1st Mission to Ethiopia." Here was the Classics Illustrated form of feminist, Afrocentric theology

Such moral lessons will not upset secular observers, she asserted, but she was careful about what might: "Here, in our summer camp program, we don't keep up on the wall things about Jesus. We say to parents this is a Christian camp, but whenever we have guests coming here, we take down all the Jesus things." As we walked around, she was aghast to see decorating one wall some children's artwork on "Listen to Jesus" workbook pages with these instructions: "Jesus and three friends went up a mountain to pray. Color this picture about it." She fretted about what a moneyed backer scheduled to visit would think of those materials, but then said, "You can rest assured that those papers will be down when he comes."

Lots of conservative Christians would not like Henning-Byfield, but compassionate conservatism emphasizes not likes or dislikes but measurable social outcomes. Neighborhood stability is crucial for economic advance, and the community around Village House is far more stable since it opened.

Respecting Those Who Make Sacrifices

From the near east side we traveled to the Haughville neighborhood on the west side to drop in on another community center director, this one with a background in industry rather than government. A few years ago, Olgen Williams was a foreman in an oil refinery and the long-married father of ten children. Then he fell, broke both wrists, and in 1996 found a new career managing Christamore House. Born in 1905 as a mission to Eastern European immigrants and Irish Catholics, it is now, according to Williams, a "secular organization run by a faith-based person."

Williams's faith finds its ultimate expression in his position as part-time pastor at a small nearby church, but he seems to have integrated the pieces of his calling. That unity shows in the way he describes his home as ideally located: four blocks from work, four blocks from church, and one block from the barber shop. It shows as he explains how pastoring and program management go together: "Sunday night at church someone will hear of Christ and say, 'I'm tired of dope.' I can tell him to come here the next morning for job training." Handing out food and teaching about work also go together: Christamore feeds those who wander in the first time, but the "second time people come they are told they have to do something: Pick up paper, mop the floor. If a person is hooked on poverty, just playing the game, he goes away; if he's hungry, he stays."

Williams's hope is that ordinary work will once again be seen as honorable: "Drug dealers—they've dropped out of school, they have no hope. They could go to work at McDonald's for $7.50 an hour, but some people say that's dishonest work. That attitude hurts everyone who could be helped by taking a job there." Meanwhile, he is impressed that prostitutes are back walking the streets of Haughville. "I know it sounds crazy," Williams said, "but when people were getting killed here all the time, no john would ever come to Haughville. Now this place is safer. I'm not saying hookers are a good thing, but it proves we've made this place a lot safer."

Dressed in black boots, dark blue pants, and a light blue shirt, Williams showed us around. His building is old, but his boxing gym has bright yellow walls, his computer lab has eleven uniform computers with Intel inside, his floors are clean, and his front hallway on two July days smelled like grape popsicles. He praised the volunteers at his ninety-child summer day camp and is ready to take on more: "I can do more with three hundred committed volunteers than $3 million." It's better to challenge people than to make them dependent, he said, noting the positive effects in his community of the 1996 welfare reforms: "Most people think, 'I have to do something because I'll be cut off.' Many are surprised to find they are employable. They start thinking, 'I can do that job.' Women are making great transitions, sometimes from homelessness to home ownership. The men are still a problem. They get jobs but don't stay on the job for more than two weeks."

Williams did not always have that view of volunteer time and work. Early in the decade, Goldsmith offered Haughville residents a sweat-equity program. He would use city dollars to improve the infrastructure if residents would contribute some work. Williams opposed the deal, arguing that previous mayors had broken agreements, but Goldsmith offered a challenge and a promise: "Face up to your responsibilities, and then we will respond."

Both sides ended up facing up, and the partnership that emerged led to a new health clinic, a new community center, vigorous crime watches, and the placement of four small manufacturing companies in an abandoned rail switchyard. Williams's demand for community involvement in decision making fitted well with Goldsmith's desire to avoid the condescension of merely passing out money like tips. Williams, who did not vote for Goldsmith when he won his first term in 1991, enjoyed summarizing one conversation: "Mayor Goldsmith said, 'You're the experts. How can I help?' I said, 'Do what you're supposed to do. Get the abandoned cars off the street.' He did it."

A new relationship between police and community emerged. "Now we preach law and order," Williams said. "We believe that the police are here for our good. There are a few bad officers, but we don't throw away everything because of that. We need the police, so we meet with them three or four times a month and tell them how we want to be policed. We interview potential hires and track them afterward. When an officer is rude, we'll call him in." Cooperative police receive help in return: "We report crime and bad activities, and as ministers we will try to calm volatile situations. We have someone an old person can call when drug dealers are causing trouble, and we'll get that information to the police. That way, old people can call without worrying about dealers getting at them. We all believe that dope dealers, whether black, white, or purple, need to go to jail."

The nightmare of kids turning to drugs has inspired some extraordinary action on the part of several Westside residents. Daniel and I visited Lifeline Community Center, a warm name for an old building with uneven floors, coming-up-at-the-edges vinyl tile, and walls wearing coatings of many colors. The building may not look like much, but it's there, and it's the only real home for many of the children who come for after-school lessons and summer camp. That home exists because of Ermil Thompson, a thin, sixty-eight-year-old woman who worked her fingers to the bone for several years cooking and selling lunches to raise thousands of dollars to buy and convert a dilapidated house into the center.

Even after all of Thompson's work, the road was not straight. Drug users had used the building, and when she bought it for the center, "they set fire to it." She raised more funds; her brother bought a steel door; others contributed lighting fixtures; a board member donated the heating system. FPA steered Thompson safely through rezoning and gave her contacts that resulted in the donation of old computers, tables, and chairs. And now she has ended up with much more than bony fingers. Now children sit around a table in her center and learn about Mount Vesuvius, drawing and thinking about explosions in worlds not their own.

Ermil Thompson explains that she labored and survived because of her faith in Christ. Daniel and I admired her, but we still had to see that her center is barely hanging on; faith by itself does not guarantee success. Sadly, many of the children are also barely hanging on. Parental neglect is common. "One girl won the spelling bee and was excited to tell her parents about it," Miss Thompson recalled, "but it didn't mean anything to them." Her Lifeline Community Center is a lifeline, but that center cannot hold if the rims of family decay and purposelessness continue to pull away.

Pastors Assessing the Front Porch Alliance

The best time to gain a realistic view was 5 P.M. (Miller time in some places), when half a dozen Westside pastors sat down with Daniel and me to talk about the changes they had seen since the passage of welfare reform in 1996. Mel Jackson, part-time pastor of Christian Love Baptist Church, has a weekday job with the housing authority. Jackson, a thoughtful, gray-bearded gentleman wearing tortoise-shell glasses, a panama hat, and a gold tie, was optimistic. He spoke of seeing "positive results on a daily basis in the properties I manage." He said that out of seventy-eight families, only ten were still hooked into the central welfare program; three years before, the figures might have been reversed. Jackson added, "The majority of persons learn that the barriers are not so great. You don't see as much standing around, as much idleness."

Reverend Ananias Robinson, president of Westside, echoed Jackson's sense of positive neighborhood change. His gray mustache and goatee, along with the lack of an index finger on his left hand, suggest not only the years but the mileage he has accumulated. He told how Goldsmith in 1998 brought in Boston minister Eugene Rivers, hoping that he would inspire local pastors to follow his model for street-based interaction with gangs. Prodded by Rivers, the Indianapolis pastors started going out on weekly "faith walks" at night to make contact with people, especially young men, who were hanging out on mean streets. The pastors held "resurrection forums" in which drug dealers and others were invited to change their lives. They offered dealers help in getting honorable jobs.

Reverend Roosevelt Sanders, who resembles boxer George Foreman, talked about fighting the open-air drug market near his Mount Vernon Community Missionary Baptist Church. As he strove to set up a drug treatment and job training program, the Front Porch Alliance kicked in $5,000 and help with grant proposals that enabled his church to buy a couple of old houses and turn them into treatment centers. "Lots of politicians make lots of promises," he said. "They'll court you, and once in office they'll develop selective amnesia. But the FPA said it would help us, and it did. It put together a team of people to identify funding possibilities. It put proposals together. It didn't drop us when the process was slow. Then, by promoting favorable news coverage, it helped us to get additional donations."

Reverend Roger Holloway, the only white pastor in the group, reported that he and his Jesus Is the Word congregation were so enthusiastic about the new urban possibilities that they changed building plans. Wearing a collarless yellow shirt, navy blue shorts, and white sandals—the opposite of the formal dress of the black pastors—Holloway described how his church had planned to build a new, small sanctuary and school on land it owns five miles north of the inner city. Plans changed, however, when FPA proposed that the church, along with a bank, health clinic, and small grocery store, build on a five-acre plot the city owned. To think of churches as a vital part of redevelopment—how unusual! To offer some city funding for the school, despite its religious nature, is also extraordinary. Holloway for his part is adamant about the liberty he expects to have: "I'll take the money, but I'm going to preach Christ—no strings that way, Doc!"

Such agreements are not a problem for Goldsmith, who has done at the city level what the Constitution's preamble asks the federal government to do: *promote* the general welfare (as contrasted with *providing* for the common defense). The FPA has not provided programs but has promoted the work of community groups that push residents to pick up trash instead of whining about it, or to tell police what they know instead of viewing officers as enemies. "A lot of us used to sit around the barber shop all day and complain," Williams said, "but now we work together." The key to practical change has been a willingness to emphasize the practical rather than the theoretical. "Separation of church and state is for people who went to law school, and all they got to do is argue constitutional law," Williams stated.

Not everyone in Indianapolis was convinced. With Goldsmith during the summer of 1999 preparing to leave the mayor's office after eight years, Democrat Bart Peterson surged into the lead for the November election by pledging to hire more police and said little about encouraging the work of faith-based folks who—when they are successful—reduce the need for police. Williams said, "Our rights are violated when there's a shooting on the street corner, not when someone is praying." He believed that more prayer would mean fewer shootings. But others did not make the connection, and the American Civil Liberties Union scoffed at it.

Juvenile Courts and Gyms

Daniel and I met others in Indianapolis who defied the conventional understanding of church-state separation. One rebel, Judge James Payne, a silver-haired, self-defined "professional doodler," is now opening up Indianapolis's juvenile court system to faith-based groups. Payne obviously gets along well with teens. When Daniel stood up upon Payne's entrance and said with the awkward formality of a fourteen-year-old doing his duty, "I'm pleased to meet you, Judge Payne," the judge reciprocated with crinkly eyes and a slight bow, "I'm pleased to meet you, Daniel Olasky." Then Judge Payne lined up his cell phone on a piece of paper, edged in the lines, and began drawing away. The doodles that day were jagged rather than rounded, as fitted someone who deals with rocky lives rather than smooth transitions.

Payne was wearing a red tie with drawings of happy children on it, but most of the children he is responsible for are not smiling. He has jurisdiction over ten thousand to twelve thousand cases each year of parental abuse or neglect and juvenile delinquency. Delinquents at the end of the century are not just stealing hubcaps, he explained tiredly, but are building adult-length rap sheets, with guns and cocaine regularly cited. It's what parents do, however, that leaves Payne inclined to declare a whole culture guilty: "We see fetal alcohol use, mothers on drugs physically and emotionally aggressive with children. We see kids whipped—I'm not talking about spanking here, but whipping—from neck to knee with an extension cord."

How can these youngsters be helped? For years, the juvenile justice system has paid secular social workers to work with troubled families and delinquent kids, with the social workers typically spending four hours per week per family over a six-month period. But actions that lead people to Payne's courtroom usually occur at only three times during the day: 6 to 8 A.M., 3 to 5 P.M. when kids are through with school, and 8 to 10 in the evening. That timing makes part of the problem obvious: "Most of our counselors work 8 to 5, so they miss two out of three, and they're not there for the third, because we have counselors saying, 'I won't go into that home. What an awful neighborhood!'" Part of the solution also seems evident: "What if we find people with the faith to go into those homes at all hours? That's a lot better than lecturing people in offices. It's the difference between telling a person to clean out the refrigerator for cockroaches, and coming alongside the person to do the work together."

Out of that thinking emerged Payne's plan to provide equal opportunity for people from religious communities. He sent out one hundred invitations to groups from various religions; forty people came to informational meetings. Muslim leaders did not respond. Jewish leaders said, accurately, "Our kids don't get into trouble with your system." Christian groups applied. They had to pledge to have ministers or other trained counselors available for contact during weekends and evenings, and to provide twenty-four-hour crisis intervention coverage. All nine Christian groups that met the criteria were accepted. In the first year of the program, they received 211 referrals. Five secular agencies, all larger than the faith-based ones, also applied, and received about 500 referrals.

Only families that indicate a preference for a faith-based counselor are assigned one—and now counseling from a Muslim or Jewish base can be arranged on request. That's vital in this and all other relations between government and faith-based organizations: synagogues and mosques need to be on a level playing field with church or atheistic groups. Payne's program has been developed with such fairness that it might not be hugely controversial, except that money is changing hands. Counselors receive a payment of $800 after the first thirty days (by which time a treatment plan has to be produced), $800 more after the first ninety days, and a final $800 when the case is closed, which takes an average of six months.

Is it proper for government to be paying church groups? Payne has thought about this considerably and concluded that "in the 1960s, the federal government drove out churches and families. How now do we get them back into the process? We can invite them now to come back in out of the goodness of their hearts, but they're not equipped to do this." Payne sees a government obligation—"We drove them out; how do we get them back in?"—and is looking forward to studying the comparative performance of religious and secular counselors. One more year of experience probably will be needed to set up a good research study. The Indiana Civil Liberties Union, not wanting to wait that long, sent Payne a threatening letter that noted, "You'll be watched closely." His response: "Fine."

Clearly, the process of creating a level playing field for religious organizations will not be smooth or easy. Payne noticed the tee-shirt Daniel was wearing in the Big Ten country of Indiana—University of Michigan, National Champions 1997—and remarked on how much his contest with antireligious forces was like football. The comparison, he and Daniel agreed, worked two ways. First, football is not just a contact but a collision sport. Second, one side or the other is advancing the ball—and, at least in 1999, Payne was in control, carefully working the ball down the field.

The difference between Payne's situation and that of school voucher proponents is striking. In education, church-state separationists and teacher unions are fighting to preserve union rules and the educational status quo at all costs. Nevertheless, the courts are showing signs of recognizing that taxpayer money can end up in religious hands as long as parents have free choice. In the areas under Payne's supervision, he is the court, and the youngsters he is trying to help are those whom everyone else (including their parents) has discarded. Maybe both ACLU-types and the public are reluctant to take away the last hope of change.

Shortly after we left Payne, we heard a story of what one group of young criminals had done and the amazing turn that story had taken. We were visiting Tim Streett, age thirty-six, minister of urban outreach for the East 91st Street Christian Church, a congregation in the circle of affluence barely visible from Goldsmith's window. Streett's blue shirt, khakis, and black shoes would not make him stand out in that crowd, but they are not standard issue where he works: the Jehovah Jireh ("God provides") Sports Club in the Martindale-Brightwood neighborhood, part of the "drop-off-the-table-poor" circle.

Streett and his wife have a young child, and new fatherhood had brought fresh to Streett's mind the event that changed his life when he was fifteen and living in a northern suburb of Indianapolis. As he and his dad were shoveling snow, young men from the inner city drove up, demanded money, and then fatally shot the father in front of the son's eyes. The natural step for Streett would have been a descent into bitterness, but over time, "God called me to work among the black community and to forgive the killers." He wrote to the murderer, who is on death row, but received no response. He did receive a response from the driver of the car and went to visit him in prison: "He had been going to chapel and reading the Bible, but he later told his mom that when he saw me come through the prison gates, he knew the gospel was real."

Streett wrote letters to help get the prisoner's sentence of ninety years reduced to forty-five, setting up (with good behavior) a release date of December 2001. Streett explained that the driver "had a job, then had some trouble," and went out that day to steal but not to kill: "Now he talks to kids, telling them, 'Be careful who you hang out with, because what your friends do, you'll be doing.'" Streett has been helping kids from backgrounds like his dad's killer to hang out with different types of folks. When his affluent church gave him the go-ahead and promised funding for inner-city work, Streett asked pastors who make up the Community Resurrection Partnership (one of the groups aided by the Front Porch Alliance) what they would like. The indirectly government-funded answer came back: an after-school sports program.

Here's where Streett once again started coloring outside the lines. Instead of just offering basketball and inspiring more kids to fixate on their minuscule chance to become the next Michael Jordan, he decided to expose kids to sports they had never before encountered. He contacted Paul and Carol Cannada, both former Junior Olympic gymnasts. Paul, who now serves as executive director of Jireh Sports, is short, black, and strong, with a neck like a bull, forearms that rival Popeye's, and the mental toughness and communication skills to convey the emphasis on focus and determination that is integral to gymnastics.

Streett and others "prayed for an abandoned building" to house the vision. A donation of $100,000 made possible the purchase of a warehouse that had been abandoned for a decade. Renovations began in August 1997, with volunteers, including many kids, doing most of the work and others donating money and equipment. Volunteers cut, planed, and padded balance beams. They erected parallel bars that would allow gymnasts to swing through the rafters. They built a floor-to-ceiling climbing wall and a tumbling track, and jammed into big rooms other gymnastics equipment and wrestling mats, while setting aside smaller rooms for tutoring and computer training. Opening day came in January 1998;

in 1999 JIREH served 220 kids in after-school programs during the school year and 450 during the summer.

Now the Streetts live next to JIREH, and the Cannadas live just down the street. Within the center, posters on white brick walls bring home the big lessons: honesty, respect, self-discipline. "Did you show self-control today?" one poster asks, and then heads to specifics: "I used quiet words when I was upset." JIREH has developed a volunteer base of coaches who look at six to eight kids as their discipleship group; the great majority of the mostly black kids have never had a dad in their homes, and this is their opportunity to respond to male leadership. Gymnastics is now accompanied by lessons in classic wrestling, which some youngsters are surprised to find does not include the World Wrestling Federation moves they and Daniel admire. (Paul Cannada said, "They have to plan moves, so they learn patience and the importance of fine-tuned technique.") Lessons on character development come at the end of each class, with everything filtered through a biblical lens.

It's a long way from 91st Street to 23rd Street, where the center is located, but the 91st Street church pays the salaries of Streett and Cannada and encourages members to come to classes. Partly because of the distance, few do. The parent church also picks up costs such as liability insurance, which are almost insurmountable for some nonprofit groups running sports programs where injuries are not a matter of if but when. (Since it has a $15 million facility, the percentage increase for JIREH's liability insurance is not great.) Residents of JIREH's neighborhood also pay something; as Jay Height on the east side had found out, poor people (like the affluent) give little respect to something that is free. Wrestling costs twenty-five cents per class and tutoring in math, reading, and other subjects fifty cents. The much-in-demand gymnastics class costs sixteen dollars for eight weeks; the standard club price for such a course would be seventy dollars.

Purists object to taxpayers subsidizing faith-based programs, but in one sense taxpayers have done so for decades. About half of all charitable giving from individuals goes to religious organizations and is tax deductible. Religious groups generally do not pay state sales taxes, and their property is generally immune from local property taxes. Each level of government has seen merit in such arrangements, and the tax-exempt status of religious organizations has rarely caused conflicts or jeopardized their liberty. Offering of tax-free status has allowed governments to promote the general welfare. If the 91st Street church no longer had tax-exempt status, its contributions would probably decrease and its costs rise, and the church might not be in a position to subsidize Jireh Sports.

The Proper Role of Government

Building a new vision of church-state cooperation rather than hostility has sometimes been hard, especially when money changes hands. Eve Jackson ran into problems when she attempted to expand a peer-mentoring program that paired abstinence-committed older teens with younger teens. The program, A Promise to Keep, had reduced the number of pregnancies, diseased bodies, and broken hearts among private school students, but officials at the state health department said Jackson could not receive funding to bring the program into public schools. The problem, they specified, was not program content, but Jackson's employer: the Catholic archdiocese of Indianapolis.

Goldsmith, however, knew of A Promise to Keep, endorsed it, and recommended an application on the assumption that the state would turn it down and a useful lawsuit could result. But when the Front Porch Alliance walked Jackson through the grant-writing process, state officials backed off, and A Promise to Keep is now receiving $100,000 over a four-year period. The lawsuit was put off, although Jackson still expects one eventually. Her attitude when offered access to taxpayer money is to take it when the funding helps and does not hinder, but always to be prepared to leave it.

Defending others and guiding them through labyrinths rather than handing out big bucks is what the Front Porch Alliance does best. It has made grants of less than $500,000 a year, peanuts by major metropolitan standards. That limited funding has probably been helpful in keeping staffers from daydreaming about government-run elephantine projects; instead, they have faithfully upheld the civic switchboard model of connecting a needy individual or organization with another individual or organization ready to offer help. The Catholic school at Holy Angels Church, which serves 193 children (all of them black, 90 percent of them non-Catholic), needed something very simple: three hours a week at a nearby parks department gym for physical education classes. FPA made the connection, and the school gained permission to use the gym free of charge, since Goldsmith's policy is to waive customary fees for church groups using park buildings.

Similarly, when the church pastored by Roosevelt Sanders needed a zoning change but could not afford the blueprints and site plan required to apply, the FPA linked the church with an architect who provided ten hours of pro bono work. When Raytheon upgraded its computers and had numerous older ones to give away, FPA arranged to have church groups get them. In all these areas, government was promoting the general welfare but not doing the providing itself.

Can and should the faith-based groups do more? Indianapolis is far from Eden. Four of five inner-city public school sixth-graders fail basic skills tests. Over half of those students live with a single parent. (Billboards advertising paternity testing show a baby with a Pinocchio nose under the headline, "Is His Mother a Liar?") One veteran first-grade teacher said her charges "won't stay on task; they constantly hit each other. They just get no supervision whatsoever at home. I ask them what they talk about at the dinner table, and they look at me like I'm crazy."

At the end of the decade, the continued crime problem was showing the limits of both government and the faith-based havens that neighborhood community centers were becoming. Police officials and Goldsmith, an ex-prosecutor, studied and applied strategies that have been successful in other cities: crime mapping, gun tracing, foot and bike patrols, and taking seriously the minor incidents that lead to a crime-accepting culture. But as crack cocaine invaded Indianapolis in the 1990s, later than in other larger cities, violent crime increased as it had in New York before the crack wave there peaked and partially subsided. One Indianapolis social worker noted that 90 percent of her students knew a person who had died of unnatural causes.

Daniel and I saw improvements in pockets, but the same question that resounded in the ears of journalists concerned with poverty a century ago blasted into ours: And why not do more? We learned that Indianapolis residents consider it impolite to honk when traffic tie-ups occur. That's all to the good, but troubled neighborhoods need more than gentility. Their great need, as Art Farnsley of the city's Polis Center puts it, is for "information ombudsmen," people like Kathy Dudley in Dallas and Barbara Elliott in Houston who can connect what is going on in local churches and neighborhood associations with what is happening in corporate and city hall offices.

The Front Porch Alliance served that function in Indianapolis, building links among churches or between churches and other groups. It introduced many congregations, especially smaller ones, to a world of funding and social services and potential partners that most knew nothing about. It deconstructed government for them, helping to create a trickle-up government more responsive to residents' needs than is typical.

The laws of political gravity, though, suggest trickle-down as the common pattern, and Indianapolis may once again submit to those laws. The key to FPA success was the willingness of city hall insiders to cut through red tape on behalf of faith-based folks. But Democrat Bart Peterson was elected mayor in November, 1999 and ministerial members of the Front Porch

Alliance did not know the type of response they would receive when they asked the new administration for expedited help.

Recognizing the political cycle, Goldsmith moved 90 percent of the FPA staff and activities to the nonprofit Indianapolis Neighborhood Resource Center, which is likely to be funded by groups such as the Lilly Foundation, the Indianapolis Foundation, and the United Way. That move raised the question: Is the idea of a government unit deconstructing other units of government, and surviving, an impossible dream? Maybe so, but Governor Jeb Bush has started Front Porch Florida, and the fire may spread to other states and even to Washington, D.C.

CHAPTER FOUR

Historical Interlude

D ANIEL AND I DROVE two hours south from Indianapolis to Bluespring Caverns in the little town of
Bedford, Indiana, and explored what promoters call the
Myst'ry River, an underground system of streams. As a
brochure describing the caverns states, "The natural wonders
of this subterranean world pass before your eyes. See rare blind
fish and crayfish living in a world of perpetual darkness . . .
where they developed eons ago and thrive yet today."

Folks at faith-based organizations throughout the country
often see government officials as blind fish who developed
eons ago. In many government offices, the perspective is often
the opposite. Religious groups are the vestigial organs of society. The mutual esteem between city hall and faith-based
organizations that Daniel and I saw in Indianapolis is rare.

Some governmental empires are hostile to faith-based approaches in welfare out of a desire to protect bureaucratic turf. But decisions reached long ago, and ideological debates that are not yet resolved, play a role as well.

Revisiting the Henry-Madison argument

Since the days of the American Revolution, Uncle Sam has periodically muttered about the neighborhood church, "Can't live with her, can't live without her." In Virginia in the 1780s, Thomas Jefferson and James Madison were in the "can't live with her" camp, and Patrick Henry and George Mason (the father of the First Amendment) were on the other side.

Jefferson and Madison had led Virginia in disestablishing a corrupt Anglican denomination during the Revolutionary War. This meant, for the Anglicans, no more tithes that were compulsory for all, just like taxes. But much was still unsettled when Britain and America signed a peace treaty in 1783. Jefferson and Madison wanted churches to be entirely on their own as far as revenue was concerned, but other leaders expressed two concerns about completely individualistic arrangements for financing church activities. First, disestablishment affected not only worship and preaching but the provision of charity and education as well, since churches distributed alms and ran schools. If churches ran short of funds and volunteers, who would take over those functions?

A second concern grew out of the assumption that, without required giving, churches would become weaker, and all of society would suffer. As the New Hampshire Constitution stated in

1784, "Morality and piety, rightly grounded on evangelical principles, will give the best and greatest security to government," but knowledge of those principles did not come naturally. Such knowledge was "most likely to be propagated through a society by the institution of the public worship of the Deity and of public instruction in morality and religion." This was the common belief of most of the new state legislatures.

Patrick Henry, "the voice of the Revolution" (Jefferson was "the pen"), came up with a plan to eliminate Anglican dominance without jeopardizing other churches and church activities. In 1784 he offered a Bill Establishing a Provision for Teachers of the Christian Religion. The bill declared Christianity to be "the established Religion of this Commonwealth" and proposed a property tax for support of Christian ministers, teachers, and alms distributors. Henry's bill proposed that "all Denominations of Christians demeaning themselves peaceably and faithfully shall enjoy equal privileges." (Given changes in our culture, this would have been extended to Jews and others down the road.) Each person, when he paid the tax, could name the religious society to which he dedicated the tax. If the taxpayer did not designate a particular organization, the tax would be applied to the maintenance of a county school. States nearby were proceeding with similar concepts. South Carolina's Constitution allowed taxes to be used to support churches, as long as no one was "obliged to pay towards the maintenance and support of a religious worship" not his own.

Maryland law similarly proclaimed "the duty of every man to worship God," but stressed that each person could do it "in such manner as he thinks most acceptable to him." The Maryland Constitution authorized the legislature to "lay a general and equal tax, for the support of the Christian religion," but taxpayers could decide the destination of their payments. Legislators left "to each individual the power of appointing the payment over of the money, collected from him, to the support of any particular place of worship or minister." Welfare programs also emphasized diversity. If the Maryland legislature passed a tax for supporting the poor, a taxpayer could have his money go to "the poor of his own denomination," with decentralized administration.

In Virginia, the Henry proposal for multiple establishment gained support from George Washington, John Marshall, and George Mason, who observed that citizens had a public interest in supporting religious teaching, since "justice and virtue are the vital principles of republican government." Madison, however, contended that churches would do fine without a compulsory tithe because the custom of giving was written on the heart of members. (The analogy today is to tipping; so deep is the social custom that most diners add 15 percent to the bill without any legal requirement for them to do so.)

To oppose the Henry bill, Madison formed a coalition of deists, "freethinkers" (who wanted to knock Christianity off its social pedestal), and low-taxers who suggested that Henry's proposal would hurt Virginia's drive to attract settlers to its western regions. Madison skillfully added to the coalition Baptists who wanted separation from much of society. Through clever legislative strategy, he was able to delay voting on the bill until Patrick Henry became governor once more in

1785, with his rhetorical skills removed from the legislative debate. Madison then successfully shepherded through the legislature a bill for total disestablishment.

That Virginia law of 1785 became a model for the constitutional framework, but Madison did not get all he wanted during debates about the First Amendment during the First (1789–90) Congress.* The amendment precluded Congress from establishing any religion on a national basis, but Madison's attempt to forbid states to have established churches failed. In the nineteenth century, Supreme Court justice Joseph Story noted that it was perfectly permissible for "Christianity . . . to receive encouragement from the state," as long as no one was forced to worship at a church and as long as the U.S. government did not back one particular denomination. But early in the century the remaining state church establishments were abolished, and the new country had a brave new way to fund faith-based activities.

The new way, complete voluntarism, worked exceptionally well for a time. Ministerial slothfulness, common under the Anglican monopoly, became rare as pastors had to serve their sheep to receive their tithes. Charity flourished. But without a constant, reliable source of income, churches could not carry out all of their earlier functions. In the mid-nineteenth century, churches sometimes found themselves without the financial base to maintain schools for all children, and it seemed

---

* One of my books, *Fighting for Liberty and Virtue: Political and Cultural Wars in 18th-Century America*, includes a discussion of the Madison-Henry and First Amendment debates.

logical for education to become a government activity. (This was not troublesome to the Protestant majority of Americans at that time, who believed they would have no trouble exerting their religious influence in public schools.)

By the end of the nineteenth century, the state had taken responsibility for one part of the eighteenth century triad of church, charity, and school. A second part, charity, slipped away from church groups beginning in the 1920s. By the 1960s churches were not keeping up with increasingly massive government welfare spending, and their own poverty-fighting activities became marginalized. But when anyone at that time noticed that two-thirds of earlier church functions had slipped away and suggested that maybe complete disestablishment wasn't such a good idea, someone would point to the established churches of Europe and note how they had magnificent, government-financed structures but were largely empty.

That evidence certainly argued against denominational monopoly, but it did not touch the proposal Patrick Henry had made for multiple establishment. His attempt to foster competition, if successful, would have ensured diversity in welfare and education. Poverty-fighting tax credit proposals today are based on a similar idea of community responsibility but individual choice. The idea is this: As members of a community, we have mutual responsibility for the poor among us and for educational needs, but we have the freedom to carry out that responsibility in a way that accords with our beliefs.

No one today is proposing a move toward multiple establishment of religion. Worship services are clearly activities with which the state should not be involved. But many citizens are not satisfied with the way the state has carried on welfare and educational activities, and a variety of proposals for fostering more diversity and taxpayer choice are now surfacing. For example, Arizona taxpayers who donate to organizations that fund private school scholarships may now take up to $500 off their state income taxes. Critics argued that such tax credits violate the separation of church and state, since the scholarships could be used at religious schools. But the U.S. Supreme Court let the plan stand.

Tax credits of this sort could create a multiple establishment in education and welfare, with nongovernmental programs receiving funds that would otherwise have to go to government officials. Compassionate conservatives support such credits, which communicate to each taxpayer this message: "You have a responsibility to support education and welfare programs, but you decide which is the most effective approach."

Poverty-fighting tax credits, if they become a major player in the welfare debate, will be attacked by both liberals who want centralized control and libertarian conservatives who want no mandates. That will make the battle for compassionate conservatism hard enough. But there's another reason that compassionate conservatism is opposed by some conservatives.

Revisiting the Sumner-Gurteen argument

For another relevant historical debate, let's go back to the 1870s and 1880s, when the evolutionary approach of Charles Darwin became popular. Yale professor William Graham

Sumner became the most famous American proponent of applying a "survival of the fittest" understanding to poverty problems. He argued that any help given the needy would mean "that those who have gone astray, being relieved from Nature's fierce discipline, go on to worse." Sumner explicitly dehumanized homeless individuals: "Nature's remedies against vice are terrible. She removes the victims without pity. A drunkard in the gutter is just where he ought to be, according to the fitness and tendency of things. Nature has set up on him the process of decline and dissolution by which she removes things which have survived their usefulness."

Sumner was joined in his arguments by Simon Newcomb, a professor at Johns Hopkins University. Newcomb argued that "the consideration due to a degraded man of any class is as nothing compared with that due to the society of the future." He extended his Social Darwinist logic so far that he wrote like a potential killer: "Love of mankind at large should prompt us to take such measures as shall discourage or prevent the bringing forth of children by the pauper and criminal classes. No measure of repression would be too severe in the attainment of the latter object."

Some late nineteenth-century government officials embraced Social Darwinism. The New York State Board of Charities, for example, complained that "idleness" and "other forms of vicious indulgence" are "frequently, if not universally, hereditary in character. Insufficient attention has been given to hereditary factors, and society must take positive measures to cope with them. . . . Vigorous efforts must be instituted to break the line of pauper descent." But Americans with a biblical base opposed Social Darwinism. The Brooklyn Christian Union called it an enemy of "the spiritual law of sacrifice" taught in the Bible and summarized most completely in the mercy of "the Father who spared not His Son for us." *Charities Review* attacked the belief that "the only solution of this charitable problem is to let nature eliminate the poorer classes. Heaven forbid!"

Buffalo minister S. Humphreys Gurteen founded the Buffalo Charity Organization Society as a positive alternative to both liberalism and Social Darwinism. He insisted that even people with bad heredity and a bad background could change, because God made all "with capability of manliness and self-respect and holy ambition." Gurteen did not attempt to sort those who came to his homeless shelter into "worthy" or "unworthy." Instead, he set up a woodpile and asked able-bodied applicants for aid to take a "work test." He gave transients willing to chop wood two meals and a night's lodging. (Married male residents received food plus pay that could go for rent and clothing; women were asked to sew in a nearby workroom.) The work test showed whether a person, regardless of heredity or background, was willing to expend some effort. If so, Gurteen's volunteers worked hard to help the person find steady employment.

Gurteen, criticized by those who thought true charity should be unconditional, responded with biblical references: "Is it not in the sweat of his brow that man is to eat his bread? Is not the Commandment, 'Six days shalt thou labor?' And does not the apostle lay it down as a law, that 'if any will not work, neither shall he eat?'" Gurteen then asked hard questions: "Is it charity toward our neighbor to give on the strength of every well-thumbed letter or doleful tale, when by so doing we are only rendering easier the downward path of a fellow creature? Is it obeying the apostolic injunction to 'do good and sin not,' when by our indiscriminate alms-giving we are destroying the will to labor?"

At the end of another century, we have similar divisions. Those on the left want to give and ask no questions. On the right, two groups of conservatives disagree. The welfare legislation of 1996 passed because those primarily concerned with the poor and those primarily concerned with the federal budget could agree on the importance of reform. The community renewal proposal of compassionate conservatives did not pass because, to latter-day Social Darwinists, it seemed like throwing more money down what they saw as a rat hole.

Once again, compassionate conservatism proved not to be an easy sell. The Democratic party has regarded the poor as a captive constituency, and the Republican party has often acquiesced in that notion. Neither has had the political necessity to think creatively about exercising effective compassion rather than merely pushing for or fighting against income redistribution.

Revisiting the Lovejoy Revolution

Early in the twentieth century, government programs began challenging the central poverty-fighting role of faith-based organizations. By 1920 most professional social workers shared a clear theological understanding, according to Owen

Lovejoy, president of the National Conference of Social Work. "Conventional creeds seem to find little place in the mental equipment of many of us," he acknowledged, "and people who appear to be rendering the highest kind of social service are often accused of being irreligious."

Lovejoy noted that most social workers did not wish "to 'defend' the Bible, the Church, the flag or the Constitution." Social workers, he generalized, detested "the intolerance of the Puritans, the odor of sanctity about those imperial forms that bend so willingly under the profitable white man's burden." The typical social worker's goal, according to Lovejoy, was to have "sympathetic consideration" of all attitudes and beliefs in order to be "of service to humanity."

Lovejoy used church terminology in a radically new way. He defined "the communion of saints" as "the fellowship of people who are devoted to something, the fellowship of the devoted," without specifying God as the object of devotion. He defined the "apostolic succession" as all who are "keen in the service of humanity." In the previous century, Lovejoy said, social work volunteers worked to improve social conditions, lighten the burdens of poverty, and reduce ignorance, but modern social workers were "dissatisfied with programs limited to a treatment of social effects." In the new era, Lovejoy argued, social workers and their allies were "social engineers" capable of creating "a divine order on earth as it is in heaven."

Lovejoy's assessment was backed up by other social work powers in the 1920s. A Rockefeller Foundation study concluded that economic assistance to families without fathers set in motion "a healthy succession of redemptive forces [that] "began to work *of their own accord.*" The *Encyclopedia of Social Reform* stated that "almost all social thinkers are now agreed that the social evils of the day arise in large part from social wrongs." Since actions were determined by environmental factors, a bad environment caused men and women to engage in activities that eventually left them poor. A good environment would save all. Compassion meant acceptance of wrongful activity and postponement of any pressure to change until the poor person was in a good environment.

Since the 1920s, social work organizations and government have been arm in arm, with the peak embrace coming in the 1960s. *Public Welfare: Time For a Change,* published by Columbia University's New York School of Social Work, typified that decade's social work theology. Authors Elizabeth Wickenden and Winifred Bell (the former soon became chief lobbyist for the National Social Welfare Assembly) called government welfare, rather than one-to-one compassion, the "ultimate instrument of social conscience in the modern world." The authors opposed any emphasis on personal responsibility for economic problems, writing that even able-bodied individuals who refused to work should not be penalized. "Social justice" required no scrutiny of individual behavior, since "the origin of economic or social need is far less important than the fact of its existence."

Wickenden and Bell's clenched-teeth attack on opposition to entitlements—a desire to restrict subsidy was not just wrong but "patently absurd and self-defeating"—showed a new orthodoxy at work. They chastised attempts to restrict welfare to those in need and unable to help themselves: "Assistance has become less a 'right' to which certain groups have earned special entitlement than an obligation on society." They opposed regulations designed to involve relatives in provision of support, arguing that any such rules "force responsibility beyond the current economic and cultural pattern . . . and undermine assistance standards." Vestiges of past practice were to be fought as the drive for universal "economic and social security" continued.

All social workers, Wickenden and Bell argued, were to unite in the push for expansion: "Public welfare agencies should encourage a continuing experimentation and expansion of new services, whether under their own auspices, those of other public agencies, or voluntary arrangements." And all roads led to Washington: "A positive obligation rests upon the federal government to provide national leadership." The aggressive push continued through the slumping 1970s and the booming 1980s, all the way to the mid-1990s when welfare rolls reached their zenith—and then ran into a political buzzsaw. With the passage of welfare reform legislation in 1996 and the subsequent halving of welfare rolls, schools of social work are facing a challenge to the government-growth doctrines of the past seventy years.

Compassionate conservatism faces a hard sell here, but signs of change are emerging. Baylor University is among the institutions setting up new social work programs or reconfiguring old ones to train students for work in faith-based organizations rather than state welfare departments. This battle will be fought one program at a time.

Three Barriers—and the Wall That Isn't

Overall, it's clear that concerns about compassionate conservatism, and the work of faith-based organizations within it, go very deep. For compassionate conservatism to take hold, conventional schools of social work will need to rethink their presuppositions, Social Darwinists will need to review the condition of their hearts, and Patrick Henry's arguments will have to be reexamined. Those barriers to acceptance are real and formidable, but they can be crossed. One wall, however—the wall of separation of church and state—would stop compassionate conservatism in its tracks if it were part of the Constitution. But it's not.

Daniel and I spent some time talking about what happened 210 years ago. Here's what the First Amendment sentence concerning religion actually says: "Congress shall make no law respecting an establishment of religion, or prohibiting the free exercise thereof." There's nothing about "separation of church and state." That was Thomas Jefferson's personal expression in a letter written over a decade after the amendment was adopted.

When the First Amendment was being drafted in Congress in 1789, the House of Representatives initially voted for wording introduced by Representative Samuel Livermore of New Hampshire (a state in which residents paid town taxes to support churches). Congress, according to the House version of the First Amendment, was to make "no laws touching religion, or infringing the rights of conscience." The Senate approved wording suggesting that the federal government could financially support churches and church schools, as long as it would "make no law establishing articles of faith or a mode of worship or prohibiting the free exercise of religion."

The final compromise wording was what is now familiar to us, and bears repeating: "Congress shall make no law respecting an establishment of religion or prohibiting the free exercise thereof." (*Respecting* means "concerning.") There was nothing about stopping students from public prayer at football games or gagging counselors in antipoverty agencies. The primary goal was freedom *for* religion, not freedom *from* religion. Faith-based groups were seen as essential, for as George Washington declared in his Farewell Address in 1797, "Of all the dispositions and habits which lead to political prosperity, religion and morality are indispensable supports."

We need that understanding today. All of us can improve our behavior in two ways. Christians believe that faith in Christ changes our hearts—our "dispositions," to use Washington's term—and not just our behaviors. But if that change does not occur, it is far better for a country to have its citizens adhering to the habits promoted by any code of morality that emphasizes work, marriage, and family rather than a search for immediate gratification. The founding fathers would be aghast at court rulings that make our part of the world safe for moral anarchy.

The fight to reestablish that understanding of freedom for religion is not a cute and cozy photo opportunity. It's a noble but extraordinarily difficult task. As we left Indiana, I asked Daniel the question that many hitters ask the first time they face a major league curve ball: "Does anyone realize how hard this is?"

CHAPTER FIVE

EAST COAST

Mean Streets and Spotlights

HERE'S A SOUND BITE: "Compassionate conservatism seeks local, grass-roots solutions to problems. It harnesses armies of compassion that tend to spring up spontaneously where they are needed, as long as bureaucrats don't get in their way." Is that claim concerning spontaneity accurate? To test that assumption, Daniel and I headed to some of the most intractable areas of poverty and crime in the nation. We started in Camden, New Jersey, across from Philadelphia. There, not far from a large state aquarium and a massive entertainment center located along the Delaware River, both purportedly built at that location to improve life in the city of Camden, sits a neighborhood called Over the Hump.

To get there, we drove by an abandoned RCA Victor factory, a mural memorializing several residents killed in drug gang shootouts, a huge Liquorama, a housing project with two-story red and yellow brick buildings, and a church with razor wire surrounding its parking lot. Odors emanating from Camden's remaining job providers—a licorice plant (Mafco Worldwide: Leadership in Licorice) and a garbage plant—are inescapable.

Over the Hump is officially called Golden Terrace, but its popular name comes from both a rise on the road that leads there and the sense that its dilapidated blocks of row houses are too far gone to save. The row houses, two policemen told us, are a rat's warren of crack havens, with guards who watch for police raids and escape routes planned out. Hookers who have fallen to the bottom of the barrel hang out there, trading what is left of their bodies for drugs. Daniel, scrutinizing boarded-up windows and broken plywood doors, noted that the kudzu poverty of the South did not look nearly as vicious.

But what impressed us most was not the sadness but the exception. We had been told that the neighborhood was all crack havens, but that was wrong. On Gordon Street, in the midst of the worst of the worst, sat a neatly painted house with a picket fence surrounding a tiny yard covered by indoor-outdoor carpeting. A nameplate said Mr. Clark, and we got out to knock on his door and find out why he was different. The answer was simple yet elegant: he is a long-term resident who refuses to give up.

Poor neighborhoods across the country generally have a Clark or two. Contrast that tenacity with a more typical poverty-fighting strategy. We looked at a press release about an upcoming benefit concert by Jackson Browne, Bonnie Raitt, and others at the glitzy entertainment center on the river. The concert was to benefit an antipoverty march, and the press release asked, "If you are anywhere near Camden, could you please let your readers know that they can get Golden Circle tickets (priority seating plus a chance to meet the artists at an after-show reception)?" Too bad the reception would not be at Mr. Clark's house. We need to honor people who persevere.

Philadelphia and the Broken Bell

As Daniel and I drove across the bridge into Philadelphia, I told him of the five days I spent there in 1970, when several dozen other Yale students and I responded to the plea of that era's public relations master, the late Congressman Allard Lowenstein. We went door-to-door in northeast Philadelphia passing out literature for Norval Reese, a peace candidate for the Senate in the Democratic primary. "Reese for peace" was our mantra. Not until election night did we figure out that Reese had no chance and never had had a chance. We had been brought in to improve the prospects of ward candidates from one liberal faction running against another faction.

Still, the experience was memorable because it was the only time in my life that I've been kicked by a congressman. I was an officially approved pollwatcher on election day, and thus had a legitimate place on the sidewalk next to Abe, the dominant faction's ward heeler. When he walked up the sidewalk toward prospective voters to remind them of how he had fixed tickets for them, I walked beside him, listening in. By midafternoon, when Congressman Joshua Eilberg showed up

111

to see how his boys were doing, Abe had had enough. He told the congressman, who a few years later did jail time for corrupt practices, that I was bugging him; Eilberg promptly unleashed a fluttery kick to my backside, muttering, "Get out of here, kid."

Nearly three decades later, with Daniel, I saw that what was a lower middle-class area then had taken many kicks to the head. Many of the row houses were now boarded up, and only the best could be praised as merely dilapidated. At spots where fatal shootings had occurred, sometimes elaborate memorial murals bestowed prestige and honor on the slain. One mural had a list of casualties as lengthy as some World War I panels. Down the street, men carrying big malt liquor bottles staggered past small children playing in inflatable pools, or sometimes walked straight through soakings by opened fire hydrants.

That was not surprising, since early July brought record-setting three-digit temperatures to Philadelphia. We rolled through the city listening to our Merle Haggard tape about America "rolling downhill like a snowball headed for Hell, With no kind of chance for the flag or the Liberty Bell." Haggard asked, "Is the best of the free life behind us now? Are the good times really over for good?" It looked like that for much of Philadelphia, where the nineteenth-century row houses remained, but the industries such as tanning, woodworking, metalworking, and cabinetry, the reasons for houses being located there, were long gone.

And then we were at the Liberty Bell itself, listening to a pudgy tour guide asking, "Who wants a broken bell?" Like a jovial talk show host, she went on without waiting for answers. She explained that people with a broken bell had two choices: melt it down or fix it. Meltdowns weren't bad; after all, what became the Liberty Bell was originally made after a previous bell cracked and was melted down. But in 1846, she noted, even though its big crack left the bell unfixable, it was not melted down. The bell had become famous, in part because of its inscription: "Proclaim liberty throughout the land, and to all the inhabitants unto." Abolitionists, applying the biblical verse to the slavery debate, placed a drawing of what they called the Liberty Bell in their publicity handouts.

The tour guide's last words were, "The bell is broken. It will never ring again. But look at it, and look at yourselves," she said, noting the reverent looks among her listeners, and the flag caps and flag shirts some were wearing. "It's still working." But could true liberty fix the Philadelphia inner city, with its boarded-up houses, empty lots, and abandoned autos in which drug dealers sometimes leave weapons that children pick up— or should those areas be melted down?

Invisible Men in Kensington

Daniel and I traveled with urbanologist Terry Cooper to one of the prime candidates for a meltdown, the Kensington area. Once the locus of nineteenth-century industry, Kensington is now, in Cooper's words, "the cesspool into which all of Philadelphia drains." *City Journal* in 1999 noted that "nowhere are the limitations of [Philadelphia Mayor] Ed Rendell's public-subsidy, deal-making approach to job creation clearer than in his agenda for impoverished North Philadelphia. Rendell had once described the area as a 'tumble-down, emptied-out, garbage-strewn sprawl . . . where seven of ten adults are unemployed and where children by age 12 develop a total lack of hope.' In truth, North Philadelphia's 'badlands' are probably the worst American slums of the last half century, more like the shantytowns of Santo Domingo than anything we associate with the United States. With their collapsed houses, abandoned lots, and daytime drug zombies, areas like Kensington, ten minutes north of Center City, compare unfavorably to the South Bronx of the 1970s."

Rendell, who became chairman of the Democratic National Committee as he finished out his second term in office at the end of 1999, was called "America's mayor" by Al Gore and a "can-do" executive by the *Washington Post* in 1994. Gore and the *Post* need to come to Kensington. Terry Cooper knows the score. A thin and rumpled scholar, hunched over the wheel and driving slowly, he pointed out the visible and invisible, the junked cars, labor union problems, and spiritual malaise. "Everybody sees the neighborhood as a way station," he noted. "People want to get out." But then we came to Bethel Community Bible Church and the blocks around it, and met several staff members who had purposefully come to the same place from which so many were fleeing.

Ralph Rosario, a student at the Art Institute of Philadelphia, was our initial guide for a walking tour of the church's efforts. Rosario's heroin-using, HIV-positive father abandoned him, along with his mother and sister, years ago. They became crack addicts who found ways to get everything (including electricity and gas) illegally, but Rosario had the faith to stay clean, take classes, and with donated equipment build an audio-video office at the church. By the summer of 1999 eight groups had come to record, and Rosario hoped to build a church business.

We met another church member, Nimo Colon, a parapalegic weight lifter. While on drugs eighteen years ago, he accidentally shot himself through the spine. Bitter and unable to perform much manual labor, he sold drugs and saw no meaning to life until God grabbed him twelve years ago. He is now in charge of a small weight room that Bethel owns down the street. It's used by forty men each week, with no payment or conditions for use except one: the men need to attend church, Bible study, or church counseling at least once per week.

These are moving histories that could make great feature stories, but Bethel has no publicist, and inquiring reporters have not shown up. The outside help that did arrive came in the person of accountant David (Coz) Crosscomb, who journeyed from Australia three years ago to become Bethel's director of economic development. Crosscomb had wanted to come to America not for streets paved with gold but to see what he could do about sidewalks covered with trash. He's trying to get things going, but the discouragement of dealing with Philadelphia officials was taking a toll on him: "The license and inspections bureau is so politicized that it acts quickly only when connections are brought to bear. Under ordinary circumstances, it takes months to have an abandoned car towed and years to close a crack house."

Union clout makes fix-up work harder. If a plumber comes in from elsewhere to do volunteer work, he needs to have a city license. Garbage often is not collected, and owners have little incentive to fix up houses when the result will be a huge jump in taxes. Frustrations abound, but Bethel folks generally see a half-full glass. Rosario took us into the building the church had purchased as a learning center from a woman who initially had planned to sell it to one of the local drug dealers. It had plywood over some of the windows and bullet holes through the plywood, but Rosario proudly showed the peeling felt pool tables, old foosball games, and old, scarred desks.

Bethel was making do in other ways as well. It has little office space, so in front of the sanctuary, on the sidewalk, medical students volunteer to give free blood pressure, diabetes, and HIV tests. When a baby in Crosscomb's arms cried, he mentioned that he is taking care of Ralph's niece for six months because, as he put it delicately, "her mom's away." (She was in prison.) Church members bear each other's burdens because of their understanding of true liberty. Bethel co-pastor Joel van Dyke said in a July sermon delivered to eighty sitting in old wooden pews, "Too many people think that freedom means being able to do whatever you want to do. But how many of you know the thrill of being a tool in the hands of God to redeem another human life?"

All that is very good, but city officials who should be enthralled with efforts to retrieve a few blocks from the cesspool were uncomprehending. Bethel would like to buy a city-owned empty lot around the corner from it. Regulations stress that the city should sell property at market value, and right now, given the neighborhood and its plethora of abandoned homes and lots, market value is about zero. The city, however, has valued the empty lot at $40,000, which is what it could bring if the neighborhood is revived—but it won't be revived unless the church expands its presence there—a catch-22, but also, Crosscomb noted, a problem of understanding: "The city keeps asking, do you want this lot for the community or the church?"

Officials might cut a deal if, like their counterparts in Indianapolis, they saw the value of the church activity for the city, but "they don't grasp that everything we do goes into the community," Crosscomb said. "The city doesn't understand what churches like this one have to offer." The difference between Philadelphia and Indianapolis government could not be clearer. Mayor Rendell had some successes in a perilous job, but his system still emphasized centralized solutions more than supporting (or at least getting out of the way of) grass-roots efforts. Indianapolis cut total spending during the 1990s, but Philadelphia's continued to go up even though its population was shrinking, and its taxes remained among the highest in the country.

The 1990 census showed a population of 1.4 million, down 30 percent from the city's high of 2 million. The 2000 census will show a further downdraft. Some historians look at the decline of factory jobs and say Philadelphia has had no choice but to decline from the time it was known as "the workshop of the world." Others blame federal and state policies that facilitated freeway building, and the growth of suburbs made possible by government-guaranteed mortgages. The apologists make sound points but at times forget that the attractions from outside only accompanied a subtraction of what would keep people in the city: safe streets and decent schools. Companies that considered taking jobs elsewhere found that the city was doing nothing to capitalize on its competitive advantages in a way that would give them a reason to remain.

Using Publicity to Finance Faith-Based Groups

One competitive advantage on which politicians and businessmen should build is the existence of congregations with people tutored in the biblical principles that make them, among other things, responsible workers. Bethel is probably too small for companies to notice, but it's hard to miss Greater Exodus Baptist Church on Broad Street, a straight shot north from city hall. On the outside are red pillars and big glass doors below elegantly carved arches. Churchgoers stream through those doors into a sanctuary with a thousand blue, white, and red seats. Above is a fifty-foot-high ceiling with intricate designs etched into it, and paintings of apostles, disciples, and Moses carrying the commandment tablets.

The church building, Presbyterian-built 120 years ago, also contains numerous offices, classrooms, and meeting spaces. As the Presbyterians headed to Main Line suburbs at midcentury, Catholics bought the building with the goal of creating a largely black church with an "African-American mass," but not enough people came. It changed hands again, but two decades ago the latest owners of the doubly mortgaged building faced bankruptcy, pigeon infestation, structural damage, and a $32,000 gas bill. They had $300 in the bank.

To their rescue came "the praying tailback," Herb Lusk, the first National Football League player to use the end zone as the pulpit by crouching prayerfully following a touchdown. Lusk had often wanted to emulate his dad, a pastor in California, but hadn't "heard God's call," and so parlayed his football talent in the late 1970s with the Philadelphia Eagles. Two decades ago, just retired from sports and considering what to do next, he saw the sanctuary with its buckets to catch roof leaks as a message from God. Lusk had been studying informally, but went on to gain a master's degree in divinity from Reformed Episcopal Seminary.

Lusk, knowing the value of publicity, gives reporters colorful stories. He tells how, early in his pastorate, when the unpaid $32,000 bill led to a gas cut-off, he headed to company headquarters and asked for the gas to be turned back on while payments were made gradually. Rebuffed, Lusk grabbed onto a column and wouldn't let go until the supervisor came. The supervisor turned out to be a football fan and wanted to avoid negative publicity; the gas stayed on. Lusk also tells how prostitutes used to hang out on the church steps, until he went out with a Bible and started reading in a loud voice, beginning with Genesis 1:1: "In the beginning God created the heavens and the earth." He filibustered on until the hookers either started coming to church or moved on.

Lusk has a look that is all business. With temperatures nearing a humid 100 degrees, he was wearing a black suit with a white pocket square, a French-cuffed shirt with big black cufflinks, and wingtips. As we walked outside, he showed us where the church is planting forty trees around its perimeter, trying to transform the look from standard-issue urban waste-land. Inside, the look is very different from Bethel's garage sale nonchic. One computer lab has twenty new PCs, with office chairs and computer desks surprisingly uniform, unlike the ragtag collections typical at faith-based organizations. The computers are from the government and are here to help women who use them from 9 A.M. to 4 P.M. in a welfare-to-work federally funded training program. Other labs have dozens more, all networked and all with ergonomic desks and chairs. Again, taxpayer dollars are at work.

Other rooms also were filled with computers as well as posters: "Attitude is a little thing that makes a big difference." "Your attitude determines your altitude." When Daniel, stunned by all the technological wealth, asked Lusk whether strings were attached to this governmental largesse, the pastor responded heartily: "No, we don't talk about Christ during the training, but we promote our offer of a free lunch for partici-pants, with Bible teaching during it." Four out of five trainees come, and some start coming to church. The church uses the government-gift computers for a biblical mentoring program on Saturday. And, Lusk said, the government pays thousands of dollars at market rates to lease space from the church: "Once that money comes to the church, we use it as we see fit. So why turn all of that down?"

Government gives and government takes away, many orga-nizations have learned. Daniel asked, "What if the grant ends suddenly?" "Oh, the church can support itself," Lusk replied.

"This is all extra, giving us opportunity, but our main focus is always the church, and government funds don't change that." The funds do help pay for an after-school program for 120 elementary and middle school children who eat dinner at the church because most of their mothers are on drugs or in prison. Like Eve Jackson with her Indianapolis abstinence program, Lusk does not rely on the government to provide the cake, only the frosting—and at his church, it's laid on thick.

Lusk took us into the bank building next door and talked of how he had once been in there for a church loan, but the bank manager laughed at him. Two decades later, that bank is out of business, and People to People, a nonprofit social services spin-off from the church (Lusk is chairman of the board), owns the building and is setting up its own bank. People to People and Penn Mutual, a giant Philadelphia bank, will sponsor a banking camp in which students will "learn about banking and also about Jesus. The bank executives are not giving us the money to teach Jesus, but they know what's going to happen."

Purists may object, but Lusk shows the running-back mentality of getting as much yardage as he can and then thanking his blockers. "Penn Mutual helps us and I'll help them get some good publicity. Senator Santorum has helped us, so I'm careful to mention him. With the Republican convention coming here next year, we're looking to get a contract for apparel, to make tee-shirts for the convention. As long as I don't have to compromise the gospel, I'll play the game."

We climbed to the top floor to sit in Lusk's study, which admirers recently built for him, pushing up the ceiling to give him a small dome with a skylight at the top, lined with cherrywood. The sills of three windows behind his mahogany desk display photos of him with various politicians. The office walls sport newspaper articles about himself and his church. But the bookcases include Puritan sermons that Lusk clearly has read. He does not shy away from biblical doctrines that are out of fashion. "I believe in heaven and hell," he said. "Hell's a great motivator."

To promote those doctrines and his church, Lusk uses connections and publicity. His earlier football fame still helps in making contacts, and sometimes converts. He joined Philadelphia's prestigious Union League Club—pastors pay only $300 a year—and when he comes for lunch peeks into a variety of small rooms at the club, telling his guest, "I'm going to pick the room to eat in by who is in there and can help me." Suburban churches are full of CEOs who eat at the club, Lusk knows; he wants them to adopt five welfare families each and develop more inner-city jobs, in the confident belief that Lusk is helping to produce a responsible workforce. City hall is full of officials who won't take action unless there is political pressure or personal contact, Lusk knows, so he makes contacts who will be helpful in "getting the city to do some things."

When government funding is involved, churches have a tendency to go to extremes, with some saying, "Don't touch, don't taste," and others crooning, "We'll get all the money we can, anyway we can." Lusk, however, has a well-developed theology concerning the appropriate role of government: "I'm a taxpayer; that's my money." He does not think that that he should be quiet about the use of that which is rendered unto Caesar. He also understands that God is God and that everything belongs to him, so even that which is rendered unto Caesar is not beyond God's control.

Meanwhile, Lusk is looking ahead to having his church-affiliated nonprofit build some businesses: "We're developing here people who are ready for work in skills and spirit. We'd like welfare recipients doing word processing for eight hours at night here. We'd have a twenty-four-hour-a-day care center, with some of the women working in day care to fulfill their twenty-hour welfare-for-work requirement. They'd take care of their own kids and others. We want to take another building just down the street and build a catering facility there. We'll train people and have a banquet room on the top floor. We'll publicize that; people will know, and people will come."

Lusk is confident that he can navigate in government and corporate waters, but he knows his situation is rare. "We need to develop a delivery system for the Bethel Temples," he said, "because those little groups don't have the contacts." In Indianapolis they would, because the city government has reached out to them. In most other cities, though, politicians follow the public agenda set by the press, and those without some fame have to yell the loudest or build the largest churches to attract notice. Philadelphia showed lots of evidence of this, and on July 4 I was able to show some to Daniel both near the cameras and action, and far from it.

That morning chairs were lined up in front of Independence Hall for presentation of the 1999 Philadelphia Liberty Medal to South Korea's president, Kim Dae-jung. Speeches by President Clinton, Pennsylvania governor Tom Ridge, and Mayor Rendell were scheduled to mix with music by the 553rd U.S. Air Force Band, the Philadelphia Gospel Seminars Choir, and the Colonial Philadelphia Fife and Drum. But two sets of onlookers were not impressed by either the words or the music.

On the far side of Sixth Street, in front of a red brick building, four dozen Koreans stood silently. They wore surgical masks marked with a big X over their mouths, and held signs—"Stop Human Rights Abuse"—asking for repeal of South Korea's National Security Law. They showed great dignity. The press paid no attention to them. And across Market Street, a noisy "Free Mumia" demonstation was going on. His partisans were praising Mumia Abu Jamal, the convicted cop killer: "Mumia is fearless, so are we." The "Academics for Mumia" emphasized "Education, Not Incarceration." Others signs pleaded—"Free Mumia: We Need His Voice"—or showed belligerence: "We the people demand freedom for Mumia." A bicyclist with an American flag in red, green, and blue Rastafarian colors rode slowly back and forth.

There was not much action, really, but the TV trucks from Eyewitness News 3, News 10 NBC, and other stations were all hanging out at the Mumia site. At the silent protest, the Koreans offered no music and no words. At the ceremony in front of Independence Hall, as far as the press was concerned, boredom reigned: "Star Spangled Banner," "Battle Hymn of the Republic," "God Bless America," "America the Beautiful." Tiny media hits at best. But the Mumians offered Bob Marley and camera rants on demand.

Terry Cooper pointed out, "Those kids at Free Mumia demonstrations are lost. They're looking for something to believe in. The press, by doing good urban reporting, could help to reestablish heroism. The model of sacrifice that used to propel people has been degraded and destroyed. The ideals are not taught."

Advantages and Disadvantages of Size

Philadelphia government and media leaders seem to pay attention to noise, and they also pay attention to size. Curious about how much clout a church needed to get city hall's attention, Daniel and I visited what is said to be the biggest inner-city church in Philadelphia, Deliverance Evangelistic. Its huge red brick building, constructed at the beginning of the 1990s on the site of the old Connie Mack Stadium, looks like a massive museum. Worshippers come through the main entrance with its five glass double doors and encounter a circular information desk, with brochures neatly laid out. Big stairways on either side of the foyer lead to the balcony. Inside the sanctuary, each of the 5,140 purplish seats has good sight lines to the pulpit, which stands exactly where the pitcher's mound was.

A guide rattled off other statistics. Deliverance has about ten thousand members, and three thousand attend Sunday school. Behind the pulpit are seats for a choir of 150. Sixty babies and their parents can find solace in cry rooms. The building cost $13.7 million. The guide does not mention that the steep mortgage almost bankrupted the church last year, giving legendary pastor Ben Smith what he calls the worst experience of his life. Smith, now eighty-five, began the church in 1959 when he assembled ten people for a prayer group and Bible study. The church began meeting in 1961 in one movie theater and then moved to a larger theater that seated twenty-two hundred before entering its current home.

But Ben Smith is known for even more than building such a church. John DiIulio, the Princeton professor whose early research concerned crime and how to fight it, took his first steps toward faith in Christ when he saw the effect Smith's preaching and teaching had on crime in his neighborhood. The dip was inexplicable by the usual socioeconomic standards. The only logical explanation was that Smith's work, and perhaps God's grace, had brought about an almost miraculous change.

When Daniel and I met Ben Smith, we could see why. He conveyed both great dignity and great kindness as he stressed that the crime drop-off came because of genuine inner change. "Make Jesus the center of life," Smith said, "and the other issues fall into place." Creating new jobs, he noted, was not nearly as important as creating new hearts: "There are a lot of job openings. Our focus is on changing people, on motivating them to change."

Pastor Smith waved his arms, flapping his off-white shirt with thin white stripes, and the sleeves of his blue blazer, as he addressed the reason for the failure of schools and many other social institutions: "They've taken out the Bible and put in guns, condoms, and drugs. You can't leave God out of the plan and succeed." The fundamental structural misunderstanding, he emphasized, was "the idea that there must be separation of church and state. . . . The First Amendment has been taken completely out of context. The ACLU is using it and abusing it. This country was built on Judeo-Christian principles, and when people leave God out of their lives and out of their businesses, they are asking for trouble."

Ben Smith's church is well known to Philadelphia politicians. Size brings attention, and Smith himself has been celebrated by criminologists such as DiIulio. Daniel and I learned that the church had no problem getting the city administration's attention on needs involving permits or police help, the sorts of things that tiny Bethel could not get done. Yet Smith's goal was not to build an empire but to transform a society, and here officials and journalists would be most useful only if they worked harder and smarter to scout out the faith-based organizations that could not readily help themselves to massive platters of publicity.

On the night of July 4, Daniel and I parked in South Philadelphia, where the famed Italian Market is looking seedy and Asian stores are making inroads. (Many children of Italy show little desire to take over their parents' businesses.) The big controversy in 1999 concerned Stop N Go's that sell beer on the basis of permits given only to restaurants with at least twenty-five seats. The convenience store owners were putting in picnic benches capable of seating twenty-five and then selling malt liquor in forty-ounce containers.

Remarkably, dozens of middle-class evangelicals have decided to live among the poor and work with them: they wanted to live in the places from which others escaped as fast as their wallets would carry them. One evangelical decided to work with the poor and live among them. He bought a gutted row house for $5,000 and invested $30,000 for materials and technical expertise, along with a lot of his own sweat. The result was a cozy two-story rowhouse with a full deck above—and above that a 150-square-foot platform that affords a 360-degree view of the surrounding cityscape. From there we watched the official fireworks shot off over Penn's Landing and across the river in Camden.

The main city government fireworks display was scheduled to come right after sunset from the Art Museum, known to millions not for the treasures inside but for the steps leading to it, steps that Rocky Balboa (of film fame) ran up. We waited, but nothing happened. Lots of private fireworks shot up, particularly from Asian neighborhoods. Some other sounds were mixed in. When "pop pop pop" echoed from a few blocks away, guests asked, "Was that fireworks?" and the home owner said, "I don't think so."

The Art Museum fireworks finally went off at 10:47 P.M., and unspectacularly continued for a few minutes. "Nothing in this city happens on time," one resident complained, "and nothing is what we hoped for." But the evening was not ruined. The party on the platform was its own success. The fireworks, like the taxpayer funds used by Herb Lusk's church, were pleasant but not essential, and that's the way faith-based organizations should regard any governmental largesse. Compassionate conservatism will have failed if it merely creates a new, large group of church-based government-fund addicts.

Washington and the Pimping of Children

As Daniel and I headed out of Philadelphia on our way to Washington, we listened to a radio report sneering at the idea that private armies of compassion can replace even a significant chunk of governmental welfare. Big numbers were thrown around: How could private organizations come up with the $32 billion that one welfare program alone, Aid to Families with Dependent Children, was spending per year when the welfare reform measures of 1996 were signed into law?

The reporter and all of us needed to be reminded that the United States fought poverty before without spending such grand sums. Besides, anyone who thinks all spending is equally helpful needs to brush up on the economics of supply and demand. Isn't it strange that growth in welfare spending often seemed to produce more poor people rather than fewer? But most of all, it was time for the private armies of compassion to stand up and be counted. After all, a study by the Manhattan Institute found 129 different faith-based organizations (64 church ministries, 52 nonprofits, and 13 schools) focusing on youth in Washington, D.C., alone. Most were run entirely by volunteers, but a third had two or more full-time staff members. Excluding schools, the faith-based organizations served about thirty-five hundred children each week, in spite of the excessive-red tape of our nation's federally managed capital. Imagine what could happen if the government learned how to help, not hinder, such groups.

Daniel and I wanted to hear directly the views of some leaders from the D.C. groups studied. We began a capital visit by dropping in on Children of Mine in Anacostia, the part of Washington that the tourist guides ignore. This after-school program has been operated out of a rundown community center since 1985 by one of my favorite poverty fighters, Hannah

Hawkins, fifty-eight, a retired school secretary and the widowed mother of five grown children. What still animates her is the "covenant with God" she made in 1970. Devastated by the murder of her husband, she pledged that "if he [God] would allow me to get up out of my bed, that I would serve those that were less fortunate."

When Daniel and I arrived, kids were cooling off in the spray of an open fire hydrant down the street, but Hawkins in her old stucco building was hot with anger. Just returned from a government-sponsored meeting about Southeast Washington revitalization, she fumed that "The beautiful people were there, looking for more. Just like the War on Poverty, money went into the pockets of the greedy. These folks are ready to clean up—unless stuff gets funky, then they call me in to be the clean-up person."

For fourteen years Hawkins, with a budget of whatever is left in the cash box at the end of the day, has been turning mostly abandoned kids, up to 75 at a time, into children of her own. She makes sure they do their homework. She finds ways to give them a hot meal. Volunteers help, but they come and go. A little publicity in the *Washington Times* brought in more volunteers who tutor, counsel, lead arts and crafts workshops, supervise team sports, and provide classes in Bible, dance, and drama.

Would she accept government funds that could give her a cushion and her children some additional opportunities? Her first reaction is to launch into a ferocious critique of the leaders of fat, federally funded organizations who were kind enough to make their facilities available to her children on particular days. Only after several years did she realize that invitations came only on days when officials were visiting and the host programs needed to create an illusion of vibrant activity: "Now I'm well seasoned. I see the pimping of these children, and I will not have any part in it." But then she talked about how, in Anacostia, not only the fathers but many of the mothers are missing, with grandmas drafted. Older children bring small ones with them to after-school care, and one twelve-year-old has a three-year-old on her lap; she's the one who's raising her.

But with all these needs, Hawkins would not think of accepting taxpayer money: "Couldn't have prayer. And when they finish with you, it's not your program, it's theirs." She doesn't hesitate before launching into a summary of her experience with government-supplied meals: "The milk was warm, the tacos were cold, and the watermelon was sour. Some of the children didn't want milk, so I didn't give it to them, and then the government people said you didn't give the children complete meals. I said I wanted to teach the children not to waste, but the government people told me, 'Give it to them anyway. Give them a complete meal, and let them throw it in the trash.'"

It's hard to imagine Children of Mine operating as freely as it does if government as we know it were coming by to inspect. Hawkins, wearing canvas sneakers, is constant motion and constant mouth when the children come in. "Get that ugliness off your face," she says to a child sticking out his tongue at another. "Wash those dirty hands," she commands another who is ready to gobble a snack. Most of the children

131

have had little, if any, discipline in their lives, and Hawkins knows she has to make up for lost time. "I ain't easy to deal with," she said, "but my children know I love them and care about them"—so much so that when she told a preteenager that his armpits stink and he'd better do better the next day, he meekly said, "Yes, ma'am."

Clearly government officials could help people like Hannah Hawkins if they would snip off the strings conventionally attached to the funds they transfer. New play equipment, new books, help with utilities, and so forth would be useful. Wish lists of faith-based groups are usually modest, but even modest help normally needs to be taken on the government's terms. Groups that maintain their independence often have one alternative route: find a way to a lot of favorable publicity so that more contributors will come forward. Tom Lewis, a retired police officer who runs an after-school and summer program like that of Hawkins, was Washingtonian of the Year in 1997 (according to *Washingtonian* magazine) and received coverage in *People* and many other publications. The publicity brought contributions, volunteers, and donation of a house.

Lewis's story is a feature writer's dream. He retired after twenty years on the police force and bought a row house on Wylie Street, one of the district's meanest, as an investment property; that was all he could afford. In "retirement" he worked as a counselor for Lutheran Social Services, coordinator of child and family services for another nonprofit, and an assistant to the pastor at Goodwill Baptist Church. But after four years he felt called to open an after-school center, and did so in 1990, naming it the Fishing School. The name resonates among those who remember both Christ's promise to his disciples ("I will make you fishers of men") and the frequently used saying, "Give a man a fish and feed him for a day, but teach him how to fish and he will feed himself for a lifetime." Lewis was fishing in shark-infested waters, for drugs and drive-by shootings made their mark just down the block, but the row house became a safe place with homework help, Bible study, and a hot meal. At decade's end the Fishing School was the after-school home for sixty children, aged five to fifteen, with tutoring in standard subjects as well as classes in computers, science, and rocketry.

And he could make the most of it. Hawkins tends to be gruff and argumentative in a way that delights some but puts off others, but Tom Lewis has the reputation of being patient with all. At mid-decade, when a nearby shooting spree left a teenager dead, several people injured, and five men (brothers or cousins of five Fishing School students) arrested, Lewis gained publicity as the man who gave kids an alternative to the street. After stories about him on *CBS Morning News* and other shows in the mid-1990s, contributions came in, and the school's budget grew to $500,000. One woman who had seen a TV feature about Lewis donated a house on Meade Street in another poor neighborhood. The long-neglected house needed a complete makeover; volunteers gutted the interior, put up new drywall, and painted. Donations paid for plumbers and electricians, who needed to do complicated wiring to make possible a computer lab.

The private outpouring made government funds nonessential, which was fine with many volunteers because they came to see the District government as their biggest road-block. "It's been one obstacle after another as far as building permits, occupation permits, zoning permits," volunteer Juanita Roushdy told the *Washington Post.* "We got no understanding whatsoever from those offices. It shouldn't be that way, especially when you're doing the government a . . . service. They were doing stupid, idiotic, bureaucratic things. They wouldn't help [Lewis] an inch."

The Fishing School in November 1998 was finally able to open its second site. When Daniel and I visited it in July 1999, the house glowed with white paint on the outside and brightly colored fish wallpaper within. Children crowded into the computer lab upstairs with its six new computers, and into the singing and game-playing area downstairs. The program's creed also was displayed: "As a member of the Fishing School, I promise to honor God, honor my parents and guardians . . . and respect myself and others. . . . If you don't see me in the streets or hanging on the corners using foul language, it's because I've gone fishing at the Fishing School."

Daniel and I saw the similarities to the KIPP Academy in Houston. Both provide discipline and love to children who may not receive enough of either at home. (Only two of the seventy children in the Fishing School's summer program in 1999 had fathers at home. Most, like Hannah Hawkins's charges, lived with grandmothers or aunts.) Both emphasized showing children the world outside their neighborhoods; Lewis's summer program included field trips to the National Zoo, the National History Museum, the Children's Museum, and the Washington Navy Yard. Both programs are premised on Booker T. Washington's belief that poor youngsters need to outwork their affluent peers.

The Fishing School, however, is based on the Bible. Lewis tells one and all, "Success begins with God, and if you have everything you want and don't have a relationship with God, I don't think you're going to go very far." Lewis measures success not primarily by grades and test scores but by the children's realization that God, like a good father whom few have ever known, gives them love and discipline, both of which are essential.

Surprise: Men Showing Concern

Religious faith is what most often drives volunteers in Washington, as in the rest of the country. Sometimes it emerges in unexpected ways. It doesn't seem likely that ex–drug dealers and cons would be playing a large role in reducing gang violence, but a group that's pushing the D.C. decline, the Alliance of Concerned Men, is itself improbable.

One of its founders, Mac Alsobrooks, explained the group to Daniel and me as we stood outside a Washington tall-rise housing project. Stringbean thin and wearing a straw hat, sun glasses, a finely spun white shirt, gray tweed pants, and black loafers, he gave us his unofficial résumé: "I was a hustler. Whatever came, came. Gambled. Sold some drugs, but I wasn't a drug dealer." (Newspaper distribution, insurance sales, and car sales were his official jobs over the years.) For all his hustling, he says he and the other alliance members—they went to high school together three decades ago—were almost like choirboys compared to today's teens. "Kids getting killed in record numbers," he said with a grimace. "And sex: when I was fourteen, I was nervous talking on the phone to a girl. There was lots of giggling, and I thought about holding hands. Today, fourteen-year-olds expect sex."

Seven of the eight current alliance members are married, Alsobroooks said, and most have been married for at least twenty years. That also distinguishes their attitudes from those of the next generation: "When I tell kids I've been married for thirty years, they don't believe I've lived with one woman all those years. They don't believe I was married when we had kids. They ask about cheating. I emphasize commitment, spiritual bond, responsibility." Seven of the eight men also sold drugs, so "we can tell them from experience that there's a better way of life. They say, 'You were stupid, you were caught.' Kids think they're uncatchable. But we can tell them, 'There's a reason they call it the system. It works. Sooner or later a blind hog will find an acorn. They'll catch you.'"

Alsobrooks explained that he and his old friends realized at the beginning of the 1990s that men his age were letting down today's teenagers. "When I was in high school the older generation treated kids with respect. When I was fifteen, sixteen, I couldn't buy a reefer. Hustlers didn't allow kids to hang around them. Now they try to corrupt them." So he and the others began meeting at a hair salon to discuss what to do: "We had lots of arguments, but we'd close with prayer and still be friends."

The group sprang into action after a series of gang killings, telling gang members that they'd like to talk with them about what it means to be a man. "Our first meeting with the kids, in a converted basement laundry room, we said, 'We're going to open with prayer.' The adults there snickered, but every kid stood up," Alsobrooks said. "They took their caps off. At the end one kid said he'd like to meet again, so we said, 'Why don't you all come back.'"

The Alliance of Concerned Men and the groups of confused young people started having two "beef sessions"— Beliefs, Values, Image, Fears—per week. "We're Christians, so we'd open with a Christian prayer, but if someone complained because he was Islamic, we'd say, 'All right, you can pray now, as long as you'll work to stick to the guidelines of your faith.' No religion teaches kids to do what kids were doing in the streets here. But you have to understand how they grow up."

The counseling program has now become partly a summer jobs program. The Alliance negotiated a contract with the D.C. Housing Authority for repainting housing projects. Kids earn $6.50 per hour, and team leaders can go to $8. Progressing at a legitimate job is important, Alsobrooks says, because "kids look to the drug dealer who has them polish his Lexus, and he comes back at six with champagne. And then they compare that to the few folks they know in real jobs, but often they hear excuses: 'The boss doesn't like me because I'm black.'"

We walked over to inspect the corridor walls that the teens under Alsobrooks's supervision had painted. They had done a clean and precise job. "We tell the kids, 'You have everything necessary to be legitimately successful in America,'" Alsobrooks said with a thin grin. "We say, 'Use the same commitment to something positive that you're now applying to the negative. If you get up at six to sell drugs, get up at six for a legitimate business. You won't make as much money, but the police won't be after you.'" Go legal, young man, is the overall plea. "Our goal is to have the kids get licenses, have the young fathers start paying child support, take them to the polls for voting. We want them to start seeing themselves as citizens."

The process sounded too simple for some inner-city hard cases, but Alsobrooks said, "Sometimes the hardest cases are the easiest to solve. If a kid's real tough, it's probably because he believes in something. We know that man is created to worship. Everything depends on what you worship: money, drugs, women, God. People who understand that want something to believe, and we can teach them what is good to believe." But the teaching is unconventional, and the alliance—like two other gang intervention programs in Washington, Cease-Fire: Don't Smoke the Brothers, and Barrios Unidos—has had trouble gaining support from those who don't see the work firsthand. Loosely structured activities developed by leaders with criminal pasts do not exactly generate enthusiasm among foundation project officers.

Even evangelically oriented funders are well aware that faith in Christ is not sufficient in itself to build a successful organization. They know that not every faith-based organization is a winner and that Christians can be as bad at charity as anyone else. Alsobrooks faces distrust: "Everywhere we go, we cut the crime numbers, but we're nonconventional and we don't have a lot of letters behind our name. Foundations are used to people trying to fix problems from an office, but that's not going to work. They don't believe that men who have done wrong would get together to do something right, but it's often those who have done wrong who understand the price you pay."

That's true, but many who have done wrong continue to do wrong, and distinguishing heroes from hustlers can be difficult. Compassionate groups do tend to emerge when they are needed, but if they are stuck on rocky soil without sufficient rain, they often die. A Front Porch Alliance in Philadelphia and Washington could give not only a voice to small churches and unconventional programs that are otherwise ignored, but seals of approval to organizations that practice good housekeeping. Reporters, despite the cynicism of the trade, often respond positively to the intense altruism of inner-city faith-based organizations but are often unwilling—sometimes for good reasons—to trust what they see. Since publicity can make or break these groups, honest brokers with experience and discernment are desperately needed.

A White House office of advocacy for faith-based organizations could use the presidential bully pulpit to shine a spotlight on the good groups. It could help them to network, teach them how to assess potential resources, and promote replication of the best organizations. The Hannah Hawkinses of America's cities keep struggling, and for Hawkins, the thought of government officials as helpers rather than irritants represents an impossible dream. But imagine the look of joy on her face if the dream could walk.

CHAPTER SIX

MINNEAPOLIS

Liberal Progressivism versus
Compassionate Conservatism

P RESS OVERVIEWS OF PHILADELPHIA and Washington
generally use the adjective *troubled* before the names of
the cities. Seeing the problems on those mean streets was like
shooting fish in a barrel. I wanted Daniel to see the impact of
progressivism not at its worst point but at its best, so that we
could compare strength against strength, compassionate liberalism against compassionate conservatism. So Daniel and I
headed northwest, to Minneapolis, the city known as a labo-
ratory for governmental and foundation attempts to produce
better plans for better living.

We looked forward to entering what John E. Adams and
Barbara Vandrasek, in *Minneapolis St. Paul,* called "a model for
the nation . . . the nation's leader in per capita charitable giv-

ing." In Minneapolis, the book declared, "bitterness and despair are not commonplace," and residents have "freedom from the hundreds of weekly anxieties and squabbles characteristic of cities, in which the average person expects to be gulled every time he or she turns around." Daniel and I certainly enjoyed being able to walk from downtown building to building through a system of over fifty second-floor pedestrian highways. These skyways give the Minneapolis core a distinctive feel and are said to be an especially pleasant feature when temperatures are below freezing.

The history of that central business district over the past generation is instructive. Planners gave preferential treatment to businesses locating downtown. Companies in the high-density zone downtown needed to provide no parking for customers, as long as they did not go over 800,000 square feet. Those in a medium-density zone were also exempted as long as they did not exceed 400,000 square feet. Companies just outside downtown, however, had to provide parking at the rate of one space for every 300 square feet.

In practice, this meant that a corporation with an 800,000-square-foot building that required no parking spaces in one area would have to provide 2,640 spaces if it were to locate instead in a depressed neighborhood half a mile away. The parking requirement helped to promote a compact core of retail businesses and offices, no minor feat at a time when downtowns in cities like Detroit were almost becoming ghost towns. And yet Minneapolis's zoning virtually choked off real estate and business development outside the core. Poor areas of the city became poorer. Bundled-up residents of unfavored neighborhoods had no warm skyways to insulate them from harsh, wintry reality.

How Not to Revitalize a Neighborhood

Grousing (but certainly not bitterness nor despair) about downtown dominance and the decline of poor neighborhoods led to city establishment in 1990 of the twenty-year Neighborhood Revitalization Program (NRP). The NRP budget, intended to average $20 million per year, was to be funded largely from tax revenue from large downtown development projects. The city council divided Minneapolis into eighty-one official neighborhoods that were allowed to propose how the money should be spent. With some neighborhoods allying with others, sixty-six planning groups emerged, all of which would get dollars in rough proportion to the population they represented. Crucially, NRP did not try to build on existing community focal points such as churches. New organizations were to spring forward.

By 1999 NRP, the only program of its kind in the United States, was facing significant financial problems. The initiative had been set up in 1990 with a $112 million bond issue, with repayments on the bonds deferred until 2000. Many expected that in the new century, new businesses and appreciating homes in NRP-revitalized areas could be taxed more to pay for the interest and provide new funds, but a 1998 *Minneapolis Star-Tribune* analysis found no correlation between NRP spending and real estate values. In fact, the newspaper noted "home prices dropping in some neighborhoods that received a lot of NRP money," because perceptions of crime and schools were having a larger effect on overall pricing than the building of new facilities or the creation of new arts programs that NRP funds often underwrote.

On paper NRP still sounded thoroughly modern and democratic, and maybe the funding problems could be solved. NRP in 1999 was still receiving praise from afar, with honors from the U.S. Department of Housing and Urban Development and an international conference on cities in Istanbul, Turkey. But public relations hands at the office of Minneapolis mayor Sharon Sayles Belton began playing down NRP and instead handing out one-page summaries of the mayor's triumphs as a "champion of children." (She was the only mayor in the nation invited by President Clinton to attend a 1999 "Strategy Session on Youth, Violence and Responsibility.") During the summer of 1999, even the liberal *Minneapolis Star* noted the political use of youth choirs at the mayor's annual State of the City speeches and observed sardonically, "The props of youthful idealism can't always be by her side." But maybe they were better occupied by her side than they would have been hanging out in some of the areas unreachable by the skyway that Daniel and I visited.

We talked with residents of the Phillips neighborhood, which begins not far from where the skyways end, and heard the bitterness and despair that the book on Minneapolis told us did not exist. The Phillips neighborhood (bounded by interstate highways 35W and 94, along with Lake Street and Hiawatha Avenue) is the city's most populous (seventeen thousand people) and also one of its poorest and most racially mixed. To improve Phillips, NRP did not create Front Porch Alliances of local pastors and others with long stakes in the neighborhood, and then invest only small amounts of money. Instead, NRP created a new organization, People of Phillips, and kicked out the already-existing Phillips Neighborhood Improvement Association, because it was purportedly dominated by white homeowners who did not care about justice for the masses. Big bucks from the public till began to flow to people previously familiar only with small change.

City funds paid for advocates to bang on the doors of nearly all of the eight thousand households of Phillips, pulling residents out of rundown brick buildings and wood homes to attend dozens of workshops and over fifty meetings. The goal was to write and rewrite an $18 million NRP proposal for Phillips. But residents were exhausted by rounds of workshops, and without as much time on their hands as NRP-paid activists, they dropped out of the planning process. The proposal that eventually emerged had some strange aspects. In a high-crime area, "the neighborhood" supposedly decided it wanted to allocate three times as much money to subsidize the arts as to improve public safety.

Because the idea of creating a brand-new institution that would be independent of local power structures and authority figures was so politically appealing in liberal Minneapolis, city officials shoved aside evidence that People of Phillips was spending money unwisely. David Pence, editor of the Minneapolis magazine *City Fathers,* points out the similarity of NRP thought with that of the federal Model Cities program a generation ago. Model Cities was based on the supposition that existing government channels could not meet the needs of the people, so a parallel structure developed by federally paid organizers needed to emerge. "In Minneapolis we don't take bad ideas and discard them," Pence commented. "We institutionalize them."

Probing newspaper articles by *Minneapolis Star-Tribune* reporter Steve Brandt eventually documented that NRP had wasted millions of dollars on items that sometimes helped individuals but rarely did much for the community. Activists used NRP funds to build a garage for the director of a Phillips program, to pay a traffic fine he owed, and to cover a charitable donation he made. Money disappeared as the People of Phillips payroll zoomed to thirty, including an "economic justice coordinator." In 1998 a state audit finally forced the city administration to shut down People of Phillips. The audit concluded that it had spent 30 percent more than it was allowed and spent hundreds of thousands of dollars either for ineligible purposes or with no documentation. It failed to pay withholding taxes to the Internal Revenue Service, double-billed the city for goods and services, and had equipment, including a computer, a television and video recorder, tools and even a bus, unaccounted for and perhaps stolen.

The closing of POP was a sad but not unusual ending for urban programs without deep roots. One difference between this 1960s-style progressivism and compassionate conservatism was becoming apparent. Compassionate conservatives work with existing institutions, often faith-based, that have proved themselves over time. The liberal approach assumes that existing institutions have failed and that new ones must be created. Since these organizations have no track records to indicate that they understand community needs, seemingly endless round of meetings are scheduled to try to establish the democratic legitimacy of the new groups.

In the summer of 1999, NRP did not seem to have done anything about the boarded-up stores and houses of Phillips and the bored men sitting in front of them studying bottles in paper bags. Phillips overall had the look of a neighborhood ignored as badly as Kensington in Philadelphia. We learned that residents sometimes reacted with murderous intensity to the "hundreds of weekly anxieties and squabbles" from which they supposedly were free. And Phillips was not alone. The Neighborhood Revitalization Program in other poor areas of the city also tried to jump past faith-based groups and invent new organizations that claimed the ability to go faster and higher.

Training for Jobs, But Maybe Not Life

The good news, amid this collapse of progressive plans, was that the one plan thoroughly opposed by progressives in 1996, welfare reform, was having a positive effect in Minneapolis. The state-level welfare reform known as the Minnesota Family Investment Program encourages work and allows officials to cut the benefits of those who won't work by 30 percent. (Some recipients are allowed merely to prepare a "work readiness" plan, and the 30% reduction still leaves Minnesota benefits considerably higher than those in Illinois or Indiana.) Welfare recipients now receive carrot-and-stick letters offering opportunities to become independent along with penalties for the recalcitrant. By mid-1999, perhaps 25 percent of the recipients had been sanctioned. Experts at Goodwill Industries/Easter Seals, which trains those moving from welfare to work, say that the recalcitrant typically are working off the books or have other sources of income, and don't want to change their activities to enter state-sponsored programs.

Welfare reform has been good news for many recipients because many among the 75 percent who do respond have felt enough pressure to enter training programs. When I had observed such government-funded classes prior to welfare reform, they seemed like a ritual dance, with an instructor going through the motions and students clocking time, wondering why they were there. Now, however, the stakes were greater, and so was the intensity.

At one Goodwill-offered class in the Phillips neighborhood, instructor Tracy Norby stood in front of a table around which sat eight women in their twenties and thirties. Plumpish and jolly, looking like a lighter-haired version of Rosie O'Donnell, Tracy wanted answers to real questions: "John would like to withdraw $250 from his savings account. His current total is $1,236.89. What would John's total be after the withdraw?" "Tyler wants $1,000 back in $20 bills. How many $20 bills would you give him?" "Blake wants $40 all in quarters. How many rolls would he receive?" "Bob purchases two money orders: one for $15.89, the other for $23.32. If Bob pays with a $100 bill, how much change would he get back?"

This was real, and the students knew that people like them, with minimal math knowledge and similar backgrounds in rotten schools, were now working as bank tellers. The students had taken field trips to banks, up to then seen as enemy territory. They had seen people like themselves standing behind the counters, earning a decent salary with benefits and paid vacation. They had seen bank recruiters come into their classroom, in the Phillips neighborhood, and tell them that jobs were available.

Norby intertwined teaching about workplace conduct with drilling on specific teller problems. ("When you make the character stuff part of learning real technical skills, they pay attention," she said later.) Some of the lessons mixed in with teaching about cash and check handling were: "Be on time every day, and stay until your agreed-upon end time." "Do not make or take personal phone calls except on your lunch hour." "Attitude is everything! Greet people with a smile. Know that you will be asked to do things that you may not enjoy." "When answering the phone or greeting customers, use the words 'please' and 'may I help you.'" "Respect authority. Be polite." The syllabus for other days included topics like, "The customer is 'boss.' How to deal with the angry customer, how to paraphrase customer complaints; grooming and hygiene as customer service."

This training session ran from 1 to 4 P.M. Monday through Friday, for four weeks, and by one Friday afternoon students were all eager to talk about how they wanted jobs with chances for advancement and paid vacations (that last item was particularly appealing). One student, Wendy, said, "I've been raising my kids for thirteen years, and I'm ready to do something else." Alison said she was excited: "In a few weeks I'll have my first career job." Cheryl Lynn, Shirley, and Winona all said that welfare reform was good for them because now they had a big incentive to do what they should have done before. They were tired of sitting around and wanted to earn money and get paid vacations. Only one woman, the mother of five children, seemed to be there against her will.

"Yes, she may have a tough time," Goodwill vice president Kelly Matter said when I asked her about that individual. "It'll be important to make sure that child care is available to her. She'll also need contingency plans: What do you do if your car breaks down, if your child is sick? Who can you depend on? It'll be crucial for her to have someone to depend on." Kelly gave the statistics on the bank teller program: one year old, sixty-three graduates, fifty-eight out working. She noted the three other training programs Goodwill/Easter Seals runs: retail (in cooperation with Target Stores), automotive (which teaches how to do oil changes), and construction skills (in cooperation with Habitat for Humanity).

All of this was impressive. But I wondered about that essential "someone to depend on." A husband would be best, and a program for welfare moms in Milwaukee does emphasize marriage, but that is unusual. Generally the support networks—families, churches, civic groups—hold the key to whether those leaving welfare not only obtain jobs (the easy part in today's booming economy) but stick to them. Goodwill/Easter Seals, while recognizing the need, did not offer the support. And, as Daniel noted in comparing this helpful program to the faith-based equivalents we were seeing elsewhere, "The absence of interest in God is glaring."

Of course, nobody expects a job training class to evangelize. But when attitudes as well as skills need to improve, and not just for a month but for a lifetime, we need to ask a hard question. Will a secular, technical program—even a good one like the one we witnessed—do as well over the long term as a faith-based program that emphasizes job training plus teaching about God? Teller training by itself doesn't require reminders about life's purpose; at first, getting paid vacation is enough. But what happens when work becomes boring and family or boyfriend problems emerge? Where is the support network, external and internal?

Housing Bodies, Neglecting Souls?

Liberal progressives frequently scoff at many entry-level jobs, calling them "dead end." They often feel that attempts to change the attitudes of some welfare recipients are invasions of personal space. They emphasize externals, such as the occupational environment, rather than internals, such as attitude adjustment. We saw all those tendencies at our next stop, the new $3 million home of the Jeremiah Project, which provides housing for eighteen single mothers and their children.

Daniel was skeptical from the start because a facility that reminded him of a doctor's office didn't fit his vision of inner-city poverty fighting. The Jeremiah Project's professional-looking package came with a textbook social work assumption: "access to affordable housing, child care, health care, support services and meaningful employment" brings about economic self-sufficiency. That is still the conventional wisdom in

Minneapolis. The Project was receiving big contributions from Target Stores, the General Mills Foundation, and the liberally inclined Greater Minneapolis Council of Churches.

Jeremiah executive director Gloria Perez Jordan explained to us her program's pattern: "We did a focus group with single moms. What they really wanted was better housing, and they wanted to take classes for two years rather than to work in low-paying jobs." ("Who wouldn't?" Daniel later asked.) "We believe that putting these women in this nice facility gives them hope. It conveys to them, 'You deserve this nice facility.' Living in poor conditions was getting in the way of their work or school efforts." (In earlier eras life in poor conditions spurred effort, because hard work was the ticket out.)

The Jeremiah Program was not merely about better housing, Jordan insisted, but values as well. Given the biblical name for the project, Daniel and I wondered whether biblical values, particularly faith in God and obedience to his commandments, were at the core of the program. Jordan insisted that no proselytizing went on: "The one required class is on Thursday night, life skills. We don't try to change anyone's vision; we say, let's focus on your vision, whatever it is. Once a month we do talk with the women about how they are nurturing their spirit. It can be any religion. It can be yoga. We're not against the Bible: we had one class on women in the Bible and the strength they show."

Given that one ticket out of welfare for women is still marriage, it seemed sad to us that the program did not emphasize ways to enter into and build strong ones, so that at least children would have fathers. Since another way out is to start at a low-paying job and work hard, show dedication, gain skills, and move up, I asked whether the program concentrates on jobs. "No," Jordan said. "We emphasize education. All of our participants are to be in school so that when they enter the workforce for full-time positions, they will have jobs starting at a minimum of $12 per hour, with benefits."

The program, however, has made some adjustments. "At first," Jordan related, "we told participants they could stay in the building until they graduate from a two-year or four-year course, and then for six months afterward. But we found out that women were joining the program for housing needs, not to break out of poverty." Jordan had to get tough: "We saw that five of the six initial families wanted housing and were not committed to schooling, so we asked four to leave, and the fifth broke a 'no men upstairs' rule that we found we needed. It was a real learning experience for us." Now the Jeremiah Program emphasizes enrollment in community college and trade programs, not college liberal arts courses. Because of state welfare reform requirements, all participants must work at least twenty hours a week, with the program providing child care.

Recently, Jordan continued, the program added a six-week probationary status for participants before acceptance, and was moving toward a bigger work readiness and training component, along with a greater emphasis on budgeting and a careful monitoring of academic progress. So welfare reform thinking has had some effect on even a warm-hearted but fuzzy program like this one. Before 1996, well-intentioned programs could go on for years without anyone objecting; now, happily, the focus is turning to results.

From Addiction to Work

Let's look at the liberal progressive understanding once more: What is needed to fight poverty is "access to affordable housing, child care, health care, support services and meaningful employment." There's certainly no reason for anyone who has those advantages to be poor, but hundreds of thousands of Americans do have them and then become addicts or alcoholics, or mess up in other severe ways. Why? The fine essayist and novelist Walker Percy wrote frequently of the despair that sometimes overtakes modern man in the most comfortable of circumstances. Many of my students at the University of Texas, in one of the best of environments, say privately that they are miserable. Liberal progressivism has little to say to those who are bursting with benefits but have such holes in their souls that they fall into addiction or alcoholism. Compassionate conservatism does offer an alternative, which Daniel and I saw in operation at Rebuild Resources, a suburban Minneapolis home and workplace for people recovering from alcoholism and addiction.

Fred Myers, age sixty-five, returned to sobriety two decades ago through an Alcoholics Anonymous program and then used his background to start Rebuild as an alternative to government antiaddiction programs. He delightedly showed Daniel and me Rebuild's new residential building with its freshly painted white walls, industrial carpet, and rooms for thirty-six people (along with chapel, computer, and exercise spaces). As we walked, he kept up a running critique of governmental competitors: "They run a program for a few weeks and then dump a guy on the street with no community or family support. The government types say treatment, treatment, treatment. But treatment is a bridge to a support system, AND THESE GUYS HAVE NO SUPPORT SYSTEM."

Myers in the 1980s envisioned a program with a built-in support system. Recovering people would work alongside others who were in the same situation, sharing problems and deliverance from day-to-day temptations. A local church, St. Stephen's, raised start-up money. Myers sold one hundred shares of "stock" at fifty dollars each, telling buyers that their return on investment would be satisfaction over the years. Today, Rebuild Resources is a not-for-profit organization that earns over 90 percent of its revenues from the sale of goods and services produced by its residents. Myers showed us the manufacturing building where residents produce shirts and caps for the Minnesota Timberwolves and other teams. Financial needs not covered by sales are met by charitable gifts.

The road map of Myers's face, with lines etched in like freeways converging, testifies to his hard mileage in recent decades. He intensely spoke of his contributors' return on investment by barking out figures. The five hundredth recovering addict or alcoholic graduated from the program on December 23, 1998. Some 40 percent of those who enter the program finish it over eight to eighteen months. Seven of ten who graduate become productive citizens. Government anti-addiction programs typically have success rates well under 10 percent. (Success is typically defined as a participant's staying clean for a year following completion of the program.) "Every guy who gets through saves taxpayers half a million. If you think of all the programs, all the thefts, all the jail time . . ."

Since I'm trying to train Daniel to praise heroes but also retain some reportorial skepticism, I was glad that he did the math and pointed out that Rebuild's actual success rate was 28 percent. That does compare favorably with typical governmental programs, but Rebuild's program also lasts at least eight times as long. In one sense, of course, that bulwarks Myers's point: a program that lasts only a few weeks and offers no real reason for hope tends to be a dry-out affair, with the alcoholic or addict merely patched up to hit the streets again. Ed Twyford, director of Rebuild's day-to-day operations, dropped out of a business career when he became a heroin addict and regular cocaine user in New York during the 1980s. He drifted in and out of five short-term treatment programs during that period. "Left to my own devices, I screwed up," he said quietly. "I had to learn that God's in charge."

Long-term, faith-based facilities are needed, and enough room should be available so that those who have dropped out of a program like Rebuild can try again somewhere else. Myers and Twyford argue that their program, with its merger of employment and a postrecovery support system, can be replicated in many other cities as long as initial start-up contributions and building support (Rebuild's new one costs $3 million) can be found. Are private funds available for similar projects elsewhere? One problem is that with all the talk (and some reality) of shifting welfare from government to others, taxes have not gone down. Given constraints on time and the need to work long hours to make ends meet while paying those taxes, it sometimes seems hard to ask citizens and businesses to do more.

Substantial tax reduction, combined with poverty-fighting tax credits, would be the best solution. Second-best would be for Rebuild Resources to receive a no-religious-restrictions government grant to build another site. Myers has not gone after any government subsidies because those would be acceptable only "if they came without strings—but there are always strings. You think I believe in fairy tales?" Later, Myers came back to the subject: "Maybe it would happen, but you'd need a totally different mind-set in Washington, or in local and state government here."

Myers is right. Offers of government aid to religious groups within the conventional liberal mindset are counterproductive, for they either discriminate against churches that follow the biblical mandate to evangelize, or they entice faith-based organizations to compromise their faith to grab government dollars.

The Wellsprings of Compassionate Conservatism

The start-up money for Rebuild Resources came from a church. Repeatedly Daniel and I had found that the impetus for a compassionate conservative program came out of a Bible study or some other church or synagogue function.* On

* American Judaism in the nineteenth century certainly had a compassionate conservative orientation, as my research into the records of New York City's United Hebrews Charities showed. That orientation is still present in Judaism, as groups like Rabbi Daniel Lapin's Toward Tradition make clear. For that matter, the growing number of Muslims in this country also have a natural connection with compassionate conservatism, given Islamic teachings about *zakat*, the alms payable once a year by adult Muslims (2.5 per cent of many capital assets).

Sunday morning, wanting to worship God and also see what one large church situated on the edge of the Phillips neighborhood was doing, we headed over to Bethlehem Baptist, a venerable twelve-hundred-member church now overlooking a freeway and facing two boxlike twelve-story, low-income apartment buildings.

Arriving early, we walked around the two church edifices: a nondescript, modernist sanctuary building and an older structure that resembles a white castle, turrets and all. In the older building, three basketball hoops were fastened ten feet above the worn wooden floors of the old sanctuary, still with its stained-glass windows. But huge clusters of balloons waited below the baskets, along with stacks of banners proclaiming "Freedom from Bondage" and "Hope in God." Meanwhile, a strange battalion assembled outside. Jugglers and clowns on stilts or unicycles practiced, occasionally studying firsthand the law of gravity. In the church parking lot, rows of folding chairs filled up with church members, as others walked over from the lots of the Metrodome two blocks away. (The Minnesota Twins were on a road trip.)

It turned out that this morning's service in the parking lot was the church's annual recognition of the need to use its mighty fortress not as a barrier to neighborhood interaction but as an organizing post for the exercise of compassion. Not that the overwhelmingly white church members merely stare at the overwhelmingly black and Hispanic neighborhood the rest of the year: Most members drive to the church from more affluent parts of Minneapolis or the suburbs, but sixty church families have moved into Phillips and involved themselves in neighborhood activities. Some church members provide a weekly grocery bus that transports vehicle-less dwellers from the apartments across the street to three different markets. Others lead weekly neighborhood kids' clubs, volunteer as Big Brothers or Sisters, or coach neighborhood sports teams. Still others visit and pray for the sick, schedule neighborhood coffee times one morning each week as get-acquainted opportunities, or engage in door-to-door evangelism each Wednesday night.

In the parking lot, a band with guitars and bongos led the congregation in a Spanish song about Christ. Then John Piper, Bethlehem's pastor for two decades and an author well known in evangelical circles for thoughtful books such as *A Passion for God,* stood on the makeshift parking lot stage. He preached that "God is one: He doesn't reveal himself with some attributes to one culture and other attributes for another culture." He spoke of those who believe they have nothing within them to make God care for them and then proclaimed that God nevertheless does—not because he has to, but because he wants to. Kenny Stokes, the church's associate pastor for urban missions, then prayed for Phillips: "Release those snared in crack or prostitution. Restore broken hearts, broken relationships. In Christ we ask for your forgiveness, for the glory of your name and the joy of this city."

After the service the purpose of the banner carriers, flag and ribbon pole carriers, clowns, jugglers, unicyclists, and stilt walkers became apparent. They led waving and singing church members in a march through Phillips, and many neighborhood folks came out to wave. Church officers and members had already been over the march route many times, talking with residents, some of whom were their neighbors. The neighborhood is now home to many African immigrants, so the marchers sang several verses in Swahili. As Daniel and I walked and talked with marchers, we heard personal stories. We heard of a Cuban émigré who came to Minneapolis fifteen years ago and worked as the church's custodian, was befriended, and became a Christian. We heard of Phouratsaphone Littana, a thirteen-year-old when he came to Minneapolis, who also was discipled at Bethlehem Baptist and is now a pastor of the Laotian Church of Peace.

The march stopped at 24th Street, a rough corner of the neighborhood, and John Piper prayed alongside boarded-up storefronts; "Lord, you are sovereign over each house in this neighborhood. We pray for your blessing for families that need reconciling . . . for those so hopeless that they give themselves over to drugs and alcohol." The procession stopped later in front of the Meadowbrook Women's Clinic, which does abortions, and Piper prayed that this assault on human life would end. But the preacher does more than preach. He, with his wife and five children, live in the neighborhood, and they experience what my family and I learned during our thirteen years in a poor Austin neighborhood. A murder a block away, three or four years ago, has changed Mrs. Piper's thinking about certain noises; now she thinks, "Is that a firecracker or a gun?"

Intentional moves from pleasant surroundings to mean streets are only one indication of church compassion. To help with transracial adoptions, much needed to help minority children, the church has the Micah Fund, started by one member who received a bonus and wanted to use it to help others; 145 Micah Fund babies (including one the Pipers adopted) have found adoptive homes. Bethlehem's youth pastor during his first year of marriage adopted a son and bought a lot in one of the worst parts of the neighborhood, with a house now going up. Bethlehem pays all administrative expenses, so that all contributions to the fund go directly to helping adoptive parents with the costs.

A block away from Bethlehem Baptist Church building squats an old church-owned building that serves as the rent-free home of Masterworks, a job-generating small business run by church member Tim Gladder. Wearing a Victory Motorcycles cap, Tim looked wiry, wary, and weary as he showed Daniel and me his cluttered workplace. Off-line assembly work (such as putting washers on screws) gives his ten employees (half male, half female; they are black, Hispanic, and Hmong; median age is forty) some initial job experience. "The key problem," he noted "is not starting a job but staying with it. A guy quits his job because, after he had a fight with his girlfriend, the wrong music is playing that day. So many people get to thirty-five years old, and they've never had a job longer than six months. They take a month off, then see that the rent is due tomorrow and think, 'I'd better get a job.' You can train people, but until they break this habit, training will be waste. You have to break the cycle."

Masterworks tries to break the cycle by providing incentives to stay on the job at least a year. Wages start at the $5.15 minimum but go up by a quarter per hour each month during the first year. After a year, employees get paid vacation, the right to be paid on piecework (they can earn more that way), and profit sharing. Gladder passionately sums up: "It amounts to $8.15 per hour, or $10 if they're fast, and an additional $500 in profit sharing. It's so important to achieve some consistency at work; if they get it, that discipline carries over into other areas, so they'll stick with a lease, and maybe they'll even stick with a marriage."

Gladder's most frustrating experience came when a stellar worker made it to fifty-one weeks, just short of paid vacation and piecework incentive pay, but then had a big fight with his girlfriend and didn't come to work for a week. "When he came back after just sitting out a week," Gladder said, "I had to let him go. It wouldn't have been helpful for him or others." But the good experiences, such as that of the man who started on the assembly line and has risen to production manager, also come to mind. Gladder's understanding of how to be compassionate has changed over the years: "I used to tell someone, 'If you get punched out by your boyfriend, take the day off.' Now I find myself saying, 'You've got to show up.' We have to break that cycle of short-term jobs."

That "break the cycle" theory seems irrefutable, but execution is difficult. Daniel told me probably his favorite Texas joke, about the Texan who was visiting folks up North. They took him to see Niagara Falls. "I bet you don't have anything like that in Texas," one of the hosts commented. The Texan thought for a moment, then replied, "No sir, we don't. But we have a plumber who could fix that leak in half an hour." That's our tendency in poverty fighting: drop the long twilight struggles of the Tim Gladders, and go for a panacea.

Panaceas versus Personal Compassion

Daniel and I couldn't leave Minneapolis without dropping into a unique institution located by the city's first cobblestone street, just across the Mississippi from downtown. The Museum of Questionable Medical Devices contains 240 instruments like the MacGregor Rejuvenator of 1932, which claimed to reverse the aging process by blasting purchasers with magnetism, radio waves, and infrared and ultraviolet light, and the Electropathic Battery Belt, which "permanently cured impaired vital energy." As we walked around, we saw "dieters' glasses" that were tinted brown on one lens and blue on the other: they were supposed to make food so unappetizing that wearers would eat less.

Many of these strange gadgets are still operational. We could sit on one machine with spinning bars and feel a strange tingling in our rears, but few people now believe it can remove cellulite as it promised. As we wandered through the museum, looking at discredited medical devices now clearly labeled as crackpot, I wished for such clarity in fighting poverty. Alas, many Questionable Antipoverty Practices still have adherents in high places. Some people still have faith in the Teenage Pregnancy Reducer, which claimed to reduce out-of-wedlock births by offering teens an apartment of their own if they became pregnant. Others believe in the Sociopathic Money Belt, which gave a secure monthly income to alcoholics and addicts whose drinking and drug use made them unable to work.

Maybe if we frequent the Museum of Questionable Medical Practices and come to believe in Radionics, the use of radio waves to diagnose diseases and then heal all problems, we can place addicts in jobs, leave them without a support net-work, and assume that all is well. Maybe we can give them the equivalent of Boyd's Battery, a metal necklace popular in 1879 that supposedly stimulated the heart by stirring up electrical currents within the body. (In 1992 the Food and Drug Adminstration banned a Solar Energizer necklace that was essentially a mail-order Boyd's Battery.) We can say that plac-ing the long-term poor in better housing or teller jobs is suffi-cient, and we are likely to find that it is for some. But some ground-down adults in the Phillips neighborhood with fatalis-tic worldviews need more.

Daniel and I also saw that Minneapolis, like much of the rest of the United States at the end of the booming '90s, has affluence to burn. How else to account for the success of Mall of America, touted as the largest indoor mall in the United States? We drove out to it and surveyed its thirteen stores for children's clothing (including GymBaby and Gymboree), eighty-nine stores for adult apparel (from Everything Tie Dyed to Sox Appeal), twenty-six shoe stores (including Athlete's Foot and Just for Feet), eighty-seven feeding stops (from Cajun Café Grill to Little Tokyo, not to mention Candyland, Candy is Dandy, and Candy Candy!), seventy-six specialty stores (All About Horses, Crazy About Cars, The Endangered Species Store, Irish Indeed, Shoelaces You Never Tie, Successories), and about one hundred others, all surrounding an amusement park with a roller coaster and other rides, all under one roof.

The happy shoppers at Mall of America reminded us that this may not be an era of greed, but it is an era of abundance, more of which could be shared. Liberals and compassionate conservatives agree that more of the abundance could be shared, but the progressive vision emphasizes the collective. Compassionate conservatives, however, look to community but realize that for the hardest tasks there is no substitute for individual dedication beyond the call of taxes. Daniel and I met many people in Minneapolis willing to give of their riches to help others, but not enough ready to give from what we rarely seem to have enough of: the hours in our day.

Daniel and I had dinner at the Rainforest Café, one of the specialty restaurants in the Mall of America, with my friend Mitch Pearlstein, his wife, Diane, and their adopted daughter, Nicole. Daniel knows about adoption: In 1990 my wife and I adopted his younger brother, Benjamin, when Ben was three weeks old. But Nicole is in a different league. She came to Mitch and Diane in 1996, when she was five years old. In those five years she had lived in sixteen foster care or emergency placements, following her birth to a woman who smoked crack during her pregnancy. No one was surprised when newborn Nicole cried almost constantly, and to the point of near-tremors.

Nicole is beautiful, with brown skin like Ben's and a face, framed by braided hair, that at sixteen will be ready for a cover girl photo shoot—if she learns to sit still. But at eight, she cannot. At the Rainforest Café, tanks of exquisite tropical fish and special effects like thunder and lightning simulations are supposed to keep children enthralled. But not Nicole. During our dinner and conversation afterward, she repeatedly popped up from the table, disappearing into the maw of the mall for long stretches. During her absences, our conversation turned from

Mitch's work as top gun at the Center of the American Experiment, Minnesota's prime think tank, or Diane's long years of social work, to the girl first thrust into her lap on Easter weekend in 1991.

That's when Nicole's birth mother asked Diane to help provide care for her six-week-old baby. She did, and she kept track of Nicole over the next couple of years as the state yanked her from foster home to foster home. Diane rejoiced in 1995 when Nicole was put in her first preadoptive placement, and it looked as if a happy ending might result. But her parents-to-be found her much too hard to handle, much too damaged, and after a year they couldn't take any more. At that point Mitch and Diane decided to adopt her.

We started to talk about what it took to make such a decision, but Nicole came running back, thrusting her head against Mitch's paunch and hugging him very tightly. She had eyes only for him, for a second—then off she went again. (Nicole has been labeled as having attention deficit-hyperactivity disorder, and although attention deficit and hyperactivity disorder diagnoses are sometimes exaggerated, this one is for real.) Diane watched the antics and tiredly filled me in on details of the past three years and the improvement of the past nine months, measured by Nicole's lack of interest in repeating her attempt last year to burn up one of the family's dogs, along with the family's whole house.

Diane has been soldiering on, but it's clear that doing social work for the first half of the day and returning to Nicole for the second gives her no respite. Although Diane knew Nicole's background pretty exhaustively, it was largely an intellectual knowledge, she says. "I didn't really take it in until I had to go through it myself. We have to go on, for Nicole, but sometimes . . ." This was true compassion, suffering with a person in need.

Mitch, fifty-one, was considerably more upbeat. Adopting Nicole, knowing what they were getting into, was "one of the two best decisions I've ever made, the other proposing to Diane. . . . This is my life project." (Diane has three children, all now grown, from a previous marriage; Mitch had none during his previous marriage.) "My project. This is more important than anything else. We can give Nicole the help she needs to excise more demons than any child should be expected to disgorge."

"But what if the project fails?" I asked. Mitch responded fervently, "It can't fail. We're her only hope. We're . . ." He stopped, not wanting to sound grandiose, but I could complete the sentence in dramatic yet true fashion: ". . . the only people who stand between her and a likely future of drugs, degradation, and despair."

Mitch replied slowly, "That would be the pattern. Nicole was her birth mom's fifth child. All five were either abandoned or taken away by the state. I don't want to minimize her wrongdoing, but it looks like this came through the generations. Her parents were on drugs, and they abused her badly. While she was pregnant with Nicole, she was involved with some drug deal that went bad, and someone set her afire, so she was in the burn unit of the hospital for several weeks. As for Nicole's father, he's a drug dealer serving a life term in prison for murder. This has to stop somewhere, and we can help."

When we left the café and walked through the mall, Nicole ran to a computer screen that would bubble up new data when touched. She tapped on it furiously, making the changes come very fast. Daniel joined her, tapping furiously himself, making the screen go even faster. They walked and ran along together, much as Daniel does with Ben, humoring him even when the game has become tedious.

As Nicole warmed up to him, they fell into a long kidding dialogue. Nicole began one interplay by asking, "Who's Daniel?" Here's how the rest went: "I'm Daniel." "No you're not. Daniel's in my class." "I'm him too. I can change my form into his." (Nicole giggles) "No, you're not. You're not wearing the same clothes as him." "I can change my clothes." "He's shorter than you are." "I can change my height." (Giggles) "His nose isn't as big as yours." "I can change my nose." "His ears aren't as big." "I can change my ears." (Giggles) "He has big hair, like Johnny Bravo." "I can change my hair." "He doesn't have those black things on your teeth." "Okay, you've got me. I guess the Daniel in your class doesn't have braces." (Nicole's eyes are very bright, she wants the game to continue.) "No, but I'd like to have them. Can I have yours?" "Sorry, no; I'm very attached to them."

So Daniel was able to make contact with Nicole, and afterward it was clear that Mitch and Diane had made contact with Daniel. Later I asked him for the best example of compassion he had seen on our travels. He cited not a government program or even a faith-based organization but "Nicole's adoption." We talked a bit about the why of Nicole's life: Why did Nicole start life with two strikes already against her? Why did the state officials in charge of placing her make things worse by shuttling her around from foster home to foster home?

I figured Daniel might view Nicole's plight merely as the product of a series of chance events. As a good teenage conservative, he'd have anger at a welfare system that used to foster irresponsibility and a foster care system that certainly needs to be changed. But I was struck when he came up with another answer altogether—an answer based on a passage about a man born blind that we had studied in the New Testament book of John. Christ said, "This happened so that the work of God might be displayed in his life," through his miraculous healing. Daniel said, "Everything's against Nicole, so if she comes through, it's the work of God displayed in her life, and in the way her parents suffer with her."

Coda: Bowling with the Homeless

Daniel and I also visited St. Louis and saw things generally similar to what we already had witnessed during the summer of 1999. Two activities were special, though. We went to a ball game at Busch Stadium and saw Mark McGwire hit a home run. The next day we went bowling with homeless men from the Sunshine Mission, a landmark for homeless and very poor individuals since 1903, but one that's newly reorganized and once again offering challenge, not coddling.

Before we bowled, mission staffer Linda Lipa told us of her work with ground-down women: "So many times we can't get ladies to carry through. They don't believe they can succeed at anything. We set up a quilting class, and all except one woman dropped out. I told her she could give up too, but she said, 'I really want to finish what I started.' She worked at it for for nine months. She finished. That's what improved her self-esteem, not people giving her false compliments."

Some commonsense techniques can help in the process, Lipa said: "We try to hold the ladies responsible. When we planned field trips, fifteen ladies signed up but only three would show up. I began saying, 'If you sign up and don't come or don't call, we'll have to take your name off future lists. Now they're more careful. Little things like that can get a person thinking ahead." She spoke also of the mission's experience in handing out turkey baskets before Thanksgiving. "People used to line up to get a turkey, then go to gas stations and sell them for drug money. Now people have to be in the program and attending weekly classes for three months to get a turkey. That has dramatically reduced the numbers, but it's more effective."

Then it was time to bowl with some of the homeless men enrolled in a program that reminds them of some of the simple pleasures of ordinary urban life—trips to the zoo, to museums, to ball games. We talked with Danny, age forty-eight, who sports a mustache and an amused smile. At six feet, five inches, he looks like a cross between Cab Calloway and the Incredible Hulk. "Strike coming in," he yelled time after time as he rolled a sixteen-pound ball like a marble. He usually missed the pocket but remained exuberant as he told how he fell off a tall ladder, hit his head hard, and almost died three years ago, then "got into drinking, pot, fast women. I ran through my money partying."

We talked with crewcutted Marty, age thirty-seven, who stiffly hurled bowling balls at a furious speed and in between spoke of always wanting to be perfect. He would get mad at himself when he messed up, decide he was worthless, and then go through a case of beer in three hours. He went to prison after receiving his third driving-while-intoxicated conviction and, reading the Bible, began to see that his worth goes beyond job performance. His wife of thirteen years stuck with him, and lately he'd begun to value simple pleasures rather than perfection. "Best day I've had in a long time," he said, "was when I walked my little boy around Busch Stadium."

We talked with gray-haired Adolph, age fifty-five, who was on a continuing search for the right bowling ball—a twelve-pounder with wide finger holes. Over the course of an hour, he found a ball, threw it, knocked down maybe four pins, said the ball was wrong, and resumed his search. Finally, not finding the right one, he sat down and talked of "filling my time with weed, drinking beer, meeting the ladies." He became hooked on crack and dropped from 165 pounds to 110, but at the mission he had become newly optimistic: "I just gotta find a ball." He kept looking but never found the right one.

We talked with Joe, age fifty-one, who has a darting smile and chipmunk cheeks. He danced down the alley, picked up any ball, bowled without any hesitation and from a variety of positions, and rolled strikes surprisingly often. He said he used to hate white people and also developed a heroin habit, but then he started reading the Bible, dropped his hatred, and became convinced that all will work out fine, because "I have joy in my heart." That sentence indicates the strength and the weakness of the situation of all the bowlers. I've interviewed at length dozens of homeless men who became Christians. I've talked with those who knew them before and come to the conclusion that they are changed individuals. That change, though, does not signify the beginning of the end of problems in their lives, but only the end of the beginning.

Among the bowlers, Danny was appropriately laid back about recreation, but would he learn to take serious things seriously? Marty showed the ability to concentrate intensely, but would he learn to lighten up? When would Adolph learn not to make excuses and to work with the tools he had? Would happy-go-lucky Joe show the strength of character to get and hold a job? And what kinds of careers would men who have wasted decades be able to develop in this information society that demands diligent preparation?

The faith-based organizations that compassionate conservatism backs have shown an impressive ability to get men, women, and children to first base and sometimes to second. Since many were striking out, that is a great triumph. A few have produced home runs, and that is more amazing still. But for most to get further, much more needs to be done, and in the face of tough opposition. *If* the governmental mindset of the past several decades changes, then good faith-based programs can be helped to grow. But so much depends on not just the letter of the law, but on interpretation of the law by judges and officials.

CHAPTER SEVEN

BACK HOME
Ten Lessons We Learned

As Daniel and I headed home, we talked of lessons learned and made concrete. I eventually organized these into ten "needs" that I believe sum up where we are today and where we have to go.

The Need for Social Capital

Money may make the world go around, but it's rarely been that way in America. Sure, we generate lots of capital in the United States, but it's our wealth of social capital—the values citizens possess and the linkages we make through churches, civic clubs, fraternal organizations, and other voluntary associations—that has made this country exceptional.

Daniel and I saw as we traveled that social problems demand social capital. Individuals alone cowered in their homes, but those who organized into anticrime patrols found that the first step toward self-defense is community defense. We saw faith-based groups that have done far better than government in helping addicts and alcoholics return to civilization. The compassionate conservative prescription for problem after problem is clear: build social capital.

Some professors argue that in this country we don't and can't have enough social capital. One of the most influential articles of the 1990s was "Bowling Alone" by Harvard's Robert Putnam, who observed declining membership in traditional groups (such as fraternal organizations, mainline churches, unions, and bowling leagues) and contended that social capital had shriveled. Those who believe social capital to be inadequate in dealing with a particular problem, such as child care, often turn to government.

Other writers argued that Putnam was unduly pessimistic. They said he had checked Little League participation but missed youth soccer leagues, checked the YMCA but missed health clubs, checked church Sunday schools but missed church-sponsored small group meetings, and so on. Still, even if the "bowling alone" thesis was too sweeping overall, it has vital implications for poverty fighting. Studies have shown that six of seven adults have significant social affiliations and other marks of social capital. One of seven does not, and that one is usually the person in greatest need of help.

What happens to the convict released alone, without a mentor who can help him find a place in society? Or the welfare mother in an apartment alone, with a baby who doesn't stop crying? Or the young woman surprised by pregnancy and abandoned by both boyfriend and parents? Or the elderly person dying alone, connected by tubes to hospital equipment but disconnected from children and grandchildren?

For poor people, a big difference between America now and a century ago is the decrease in social capital available for them to tap. The records from old groups in the stacks of the Library of Congress show that most poor people then could readily be connected with social, fraternal, or ethnic groups. Leaders of these groups were not magicians, but at least they could keep, say, a pregnant and depressed teenager from bawling alone.

Judge Payne's attempt in Indianapolis to connect troubled families with faith-based mentors, and Prison Fellowship's attempt to do the same at the Jester II lockup near Houston are attempts to encourage diversity in social services. They are also more than that. Each mentor is part of a church, and if the juvenile delinquent or ex-con becomes involved with a church, new social capital is created.

Daniel and I came out of our trip wanting to increase deliberate attempts to build social capital. Government programs can redistribute income, but they rarely help to build social capital. But what if, when people come into government offices, they are given not a list of goods and services that government offers, but a list of groups, from various religions and ideologies, to which they can be connected? Officials need to learn what administrators at Philadelphia's city hall apparently had not learned: when an inner-city church, synagogue, or mosque builds social capital, a city becomes stronger.

The Need for Churches and
Other Religious Groups

The 1950s emphasis on "attending the church of your choice" has been made fun of on theological grounds, but it was sociologically important. Research by David Larson of the National Institute for Healthcare Research suggests that individual participation in a church, synagogue, or mosque cuts the propensity to crime, unmarried pregnancies, and other disruptive activities by 50 percent. This was understood (without benefit of social science) by many local judges through the 1950s, who would informally assign present or potential troublemakers to the care of faith-based organizations in their neighborhoods.

In the 1960s, however, a curious interpretation of the First Amendment's religion clauses became dominant. Washington began bankrolling many programs that marginalized God and demanded that staffers and volunteers check their religion at the door. Officials froze out faith-based programs that offered spiritual as well as material help. Even licensing, the government's seal of approval, could readily be withheld from an organization whose counselors believed strongly enough in their faith to share it with strangers.

Government funds could be used by religious groups, but only if they set up religion-less government look-alikes that were rarely effective. With many first-rate programs out of bounds, government often bought into the second rate. No rational business leader trying to develop an effective product would eliminate from consideration many of the most impressive prototypes. But those hostile to religion succeeded in fostering an interpretation of the First Amendment that banned religion from the public square, even though that was certainly not the intent of the amendment's framers.

Even Thomas Jefferson, who was not involved in the Constitution-framing discussions but spoke his piece later, would be surprised to learn that, in his name, conversations about spiritual matters had to be censored. How has it come about that any activity funded by the government must be conducted as if atheism were the established religion? Why do we tolerate such bias against a vital dimension of our existence that has demonstrably made a difference in the lives of millions?

We do so because of a river of suspicion that runs through the heart of many communities. Some citizens are deeply religious, but others fear that faith in God is not a key part of the solution to what ails America, but a major part of the problem. That fear became obvious again after the April 1999 Columbine High School killings in Colorado, when *Wall Street Journal* columnist Peggy Noonan observed that "a gun and a Bible have a few things in common. Both are small, black, have an immediate heft and are dangerous—the first to life, the second to the culture of death." She quoted a radio talk show caller who said the killers "were sick and sad, and if a teacher had talked to one of them and said, 'Listen, there's a way out, there really is love out there that will never stop loving you, there's a real God and I want to be able to talk to you about him'—if that teacher had intervened that way, he would have been hauled into court."

The next day, the *Wall Street Journal* printed a letter in response: "I profoundly wish Peggy Noonan were right, [but] have we forgotten Jim Jones of Jonestown, who convinced parents that it was God's will to put cyanide into their children's Kool-Aid? Or the killing in the Balkans, where weapons are being blessed by priests?" That's the way it always is. Mention something positive done in the name of God, and someone will always mention something negative. In November 1999, a *Washington Post* reporter visited the faith-based prison experiment near Houston and concluded that prisoners "seemed calmer, happier and more hopeful about their future. But it was also clear the program teaches that the only path to this better future is a fundamentalist Christian conversion." There's always a *but*. Our national impasse over gun control is minor compared to our impasse over God control.

Given the river of suspicion, our tendency since the 1960s has been to minimize religion's public role. That has worked in one sense. Government officials have frequently been able to say, "There was no use of government property or funds by any religious group on MY watch." But was that truly playing it safe, except in the narrowest fashion? In 1999, was there no connection between the Bible on the back burner and the fires in our schools?

These questions go beyond school crises. Why is it terrible for a welfare caseworker to tell a person who considers himself worthless, "Listen, there's a way out. There really is love out there that will never stop loving you. There's a real God, and I want to be able to talk to you about him"? The river of suspicion surges over such a comment, and the concern of those who would haul into court a caseworker who spoke that way is based on a legitimate fear: What if a desperate person applies for financial help and has religious doctrine shoved down his throat? And what if government workers go beyond offering access to any religion of choice, to the point of proselytizing for a particular faith?

Last year Vice President Al Gore provided an example of how deep the fear goes. In a post-Columbine speech at a Salvation Army center in Atlanta, Gore pledged that church groups "will be integral to the policies set forth in my administration." He noted that overcoming poverty-related problems "takes something more than money or assistance—it requires an inner discipline and courage, deep within the individual. I believe that faith in itself is sometimes essential to spark a personal transformation—and to keep that person from falling back into addiction, delinquency, or dependency."

So far, so good. The vice president also said he wanted "concrete actions to clear bureaucratic hurdles out of the way of these good men and women who are helping to solve our problems." He went on to compare "self-perpetuating" bureaucracies that care largely about "professional credentialism" with faith-based organizations that show "one-to-one caring, respect and commitment that save lives." All that sounded great, and it got even better. Gore talked about "Herlinda," who was able to get a job because she changed her worldview after a woman "mentored her through prayer and Bible study." He spoke of a former-drug addict, "Vicki," who needed religious conversion to "pry open the vise grip of drug addiction." It seemed that Gore or his aides had done some pavement pounding and listening themselves.

But then the vice president fell into a massive contradiction. He said he wanted government to support the life-changing programs that had helped Herlinda and Vicki, but he also opposed government funds going to any organization that engaged in "proselytizing." Curious: the *Oxford English Dictionary* defines *proselytizing* as the making of a proselyte—"one who has come over from one opinion, belief, creed, or party to another; a convert." That's exactly what happened to Herlinda and Vicki, so it would seem that Gore should welcome more conversions. Some said the vice president offered illogic out of political necessity—and he certainly had to be careful not to offend some of his highly secularized core supporters. But the river of suspicion, even after Columbine, was running so high that many reporters and Gore staffers glossed over the contradiction between praising change brought about by conversion and removing the engines of those who helped to bring about such change.

In Austin, Governor Bush did not have to look far to see the damage produced by the river of suspicion. An organization elegantly named HOBO—Helping Our Brothers Out—had started up a mile or so from the Governor's Mansion in 1987. Homeless men could get food and clothing while being exposed to some Bible study and prayer. The program was small and often crude, but it did some good. In 1989 and 1990, however, the HOBO board of directors faced a choice: remain a financially challenged, Bible-based organization, as director John Porterfield put it, or accept "grants that we could just pick up. We knew there were strings attached, but . . . the money was there in our hands, the only question was whether we should put it in our pockets."

The decision was difficult for those who had become involved in poverty fighting because they cared about both body and soul: take the money so as to provide housing for homeless folks, or turn it down so as to continue to provide them with spiritual help. HOBO leaders chose to take the government money and drop their ministry orientation. Soon HOBO sported legal services, a health clinic, afternoon Sharon Stone movies for homeless men, and hot and cold showers—everything that could enable an addict or alcoholic to remain homeless. All that was gone was the pressure to change. To get help the HOBO board believed was vital, the organization had compromised its core values. Not surprisingly, volunteer help decreased, the organization became ineffective, and HOBO closed its doors in 1999.

That year, Governor Bush took a position very different than that of Al Gore. He said that if an organization had a successful-enough track record to receive taxpayers' funds for some of its activities, he would want to provide those without demanding a ban on worship services and other direct proselytizing functions; those could be paid for by private funds. He stressed that "we will never ask an organization to compromise its core values and spiritual mission to get the help it needs." He pledged to "change the laws and regulations that hamper the cooperation of government and private institutions. . . . If I am president, federal workers in every department of my administration will know that we value effectiveness over red tape and regulation."

But what about the legitimate concern about religious choice being taken away and compulsory indoctrination substituted? That concern can be dealt with in two ways. One is to ban any serious religious presence. The other is to make taxpayer funds available to a diversity of antipoverty groups, so that recipients can choose from a variety of religious or nonreligious traditions. (With the freedom to choose or reject services from a faith-based organization, religion never has to be forced on clients.)

Our country has tried the first approach, only to discover that the absence of religion does not make a site neutral; it makes it naked. It's time to have a new attitude based on the desire to promote diversity not by banning religion, but by encouraging many beliefs to compete. Compassionate conservatives know that in a pluralistic society, "faith-based" cannot be code for "Christian." Islamic, Jewish, Buddhist, and other faith-based groups all need running room, if compassionate conservatism is to be politically successful and constitutionally valid.

A favorable view of competition has been the base of this country's economic advance, and it was the base of the innovations in Indianapolis that Daniel and I saw. The attitude in Mayor Goldsmith's administration cut across the bureaucratic grain. Instead of adding hampering rules and regulations, the goal was to get rid of them. Instead of frustrating the hopes of religious schools, the city let them use park facilities and buildings. Instead of letting no-longer-needed city buildings sit idle, the city turned them over to faith-based organizations that could maximize their use. The key was to see these groups as solution providers, not problems. But in most other cities, the river of suspicion ran high.

The Need for Charitable Choice, Rightly Understood

The first attempt in recent years to lower that river came in 1996, when Senator John Ashcroft and others successfully placed a "charitable choice" provision within the welfare reform legislation signed into law by President Clinton. The provision allowed faith-based organizations to contract (or accept vouchers) for many federally paid social services programs on the same basis as any other provider. The idea was to avoid impairing the religious character of these organizations, but there was a catch. As originally reported in the press—and this was my initial understanding as well—the law meant that organizations engaged in "sectarian worship, instruction, or proselytization" cannot be funded. In practice, this would mean that only those who say worship and evangelism are not central to their task could receive funding.

If that's all charitable choice is, very little will change. Religious leaders who take worship and evangelism seriously will remember the tales of government interference that are passed around; Daniel and I heard them from Kathy Dudley and Ben Beltzer in Dallas, and from their counterparts in other cities. Those who see the Bible or the Koran as the keys to productive and joyful life will not agree to a nonproselytizing clause. Believing it is extraordinarily selfish not to share the understanding they have gained, they will have nothing to do with a governmental body that commands their silence. That attitude among faith-based leaders will be convenient for the American Civil Liberties Union, which will have fewer court battles to fight. The river of suspicion will continue to be impassable.

But the interpretation put forth by the authors of the provision, Senator Ashcroft and University of Missouri law professor Carl Esbeck, is very different. Their understanding is that their measure allows worship, instruction, and proselytizing to go on and even be intermingled with provision of government-funded social services, as long as those specific activities are privately funded. In the Ashcroft vision, a program like Teen Challenge that saves taxpayers millions of dollars by helping addicts go straight (instead of straight to criminal activities and then prison) may receive funding to help with rent, utilities, meals, and such costs. Private funds can pay for counselors, Bible study materials, and so on.

Expansion and reform of the charitable choice provision (which now applies solely to welfare-related services) is on the congressional agenda. Senator Ashcroft hopes to extend it to every major area of federal social services, including drug treatment, homeless programs, housing, juvenile services, and sexual abstinence education. It's likely that the Supreme Court will eventually step in to decide how far charitable choice can reach. Esbeck's analysis of precedents leaves him confident that the Supreme Court will support an expansive view. Such a decision would be popular neither with the

ACLU nor with the many faith-based groups used to yelling (with historical evidence) that government funds are "UNCLEAN! UNCLEAN!" The ACLU fears that religious groups, like giant octopi, will envelop innocent bystanders. The faith-based organizations fear that government agencies, like were-wolves, will bite deep and turn once-effective groups into mirror images of government—professionalized, bureaucratized, and essentially secularized.

Church opponents of potentially entangling alliances have history on their side. It's sensible at this point to doubt the ability of Washington to shoot straight on social welfare. Officials who admire from afar the addiction-fighting prowess of faith-based programs have often shown both arrogance and naiveté. They have offered barrels of cash on the condition that programs throw overboard the engine that propelled them. So it is reasonable to ask: Can government change its spots and promote faith-based groups without interference? Or does government, as it hands out gold, have the reverse Midas touch concerning anything more precious than gold?

The answers depends on who is in charge of the government. It is likely that in a Democratic administration churches will be seen as appendages of the state. Over the past three decades, many faith-based organizations have been tempted to gain government funds by losing their theological distinctiveness. Many have succumbed. Apart from a practice of charitable choice that allows religious liberty to faith-based organizations, many will remain in a lose-lose situation. They will either enter into a halfway covenant with corruption, or they will care enough about God's commands to steer clear, and then struggle along without sufficient funds to reach their potential in aiding the poor. Charitable choice under the Aschroft interpretation could create for them a new option. Instead of either shunning all government contact or engaging in a tight embrace, they now can try an arms-length handshake.

We should also remember that not all funding mechanisms are created equal. We should prefer means to help faith-based organizations that limit the danger of government intrusion. For example, the clause of the 1996 charitable choice legislation that prohibits federal money from being "expended for sectarian worship, instruction, or proselytization" does not pertain to vouchers. Carl Esbeck points out that the Supreme Court has consistently ruled that when recipients of vouchers have free choice in selecting the provider of a social service, religious or not, the establishment clause of the First Amendment is not a concern, even if the benefit indirectly advances religion. In many situations, voucher systems will be safer than direct grants.

The Need for Charitable Choices for Individuals

While making speeches on poverty fighting over the past five years, I've asked thousands of people in audiences the following question: If you were given $500 that you had to send on to some poverty-fighting organization, would you send the money to the Department of Health and Human Services in Washington? The response: Virtually always no. And few would send the money to state or local governments either.

Almost all would send that $500 to a religious or other non-profit charity.

If we wish to proceed that way as individuals, why don't we do so as a culture? Given the concerns that both secularists and faith-based leaders have about government's making grants to groups, another means of increasing diversity by helping faith-based organizations is coming to the fore. We can call it "charitable choices"—the use of poverty-fighting tax credits that will allow taxpayers to send money directly to the poverty-fighting group of their choice and take those expenditures off their taxes. (This is more powerful than a deduction, which allows taxpayers to subtract expenditures from taxable income.)

Under such a plan, antipoverty groups will be connected directly to taxpayers. Decisions about where funds shall go will no longer be a function of political struggles over the budgets of government agencies, but will result from the choices of millions of individual donors. (Ideally, the amount of money allocated to governmental welfare programs would also decrease, dollar for dollar, as the private, taxpayer-chosen programs were enabled to grow.)

Taxpayers, of course, can already contribute to antipoverty groups, but so much money is now drained into taxes that many families have little left to give. People respond to my informal survey as they do, in part because they would like to give more, in part because we value consumer choice highly, and in part because of a sense of government/private imbalance in social services. Four decades ago economist John Kenneth Galbraith wrote in his book *The Affluent Society* about poorly funded governmental programs amid private affluence. Now many government welfare programs are awash with cash (as the number of welfare families has been cut in half), but good private and religious charities are dramatically underfunded.

Tax credit plans, like charitable choice itself, face cannons to their right and to their left. Many conservatives argue for simply reducing taxes and allowing individuals to spend the money as they see fit. Conservatives also raise issues of practicality: Could eligibility for tax credits be restricted to those organizations that are actually engaged in fighting poverty and its associated pathologies? Wouldn't some money go to lobbying groups? Couldn't such a plan give more power to government? After all, government officials would have to write and apply regulations concerning tax credits, and that authority potentially could allow a state agency to exclude organizations that it did not favor for ideological, theological, or political reasons. Some organizations might change what they do and the way they do it in order to conform to the regulatory standards.

Meanwhile, liberals worry that a tax credit system would open the doors to corruption. Wouldn't some people, they ask, use tax credit incentives to send funds to phony, needless, or simply ineffective projects? Aren't professional social service executives better evaluators of organizations than amateurs? What if some areas are underserved, or some unpopular causes underfunded? Doesn't Uncle Sam know best?

There are dozens of reasons not to go ahead with charitable choice or charitable choices. Ideologues orate them convincingly, and those rightfully concerned about the dangers of church involvement with government note them passionately. But as Reverend Mel Jackson in Indianapolis noted, "When people who are further away from the problem get their feet to the fire, a lot of that rhetoric disappears." When people see the good that small, struggling faith-based organizations do, and how much more they could do with greater resources, they tend to answer the question, "And why not do more?" with an imperative: We must find a way to do more.

It's not enough for those who oppose such measures to point out the dangers. They should suggest practical alternatives, or else we are abandoning at least one more generation of Americans.

A great movie from 1984, *The Right Stuff,* depicts astronaut Alan Shepard as a 1950s navy aviator landing a jet on the heaving deck of an aircraft carrier. Two comic, seasick government officials (one tall, one short) are waiting to offer him the opportunity to volunteer for America's new space program. "It's an extremely hazardous undertaking," one says, "in fact it's so hazardous that if you decide against it, it will be in no way held against you." The actor playing Shepard replies, "Sounds dangerous." The two officials respond in unison, "Very dangerous." Shepard says, "Count me in."

My sense is that an overwhelming majority of Americans generally and church leaders specifically, if informed about the freedom for religion that could be gained through allowing for charitable choice and charitable choices measures, will say, "Count me in." But they need to be informed and inspired, because overcoming current suspicions and the historical burdens outlined in chapter 4 will not be easy. And they need to understand that tax credits are preferable to vouchers, and vouchers preferable to direct grants: our emphasis should be on diversity, not dictation from Washington. But in a good administration, given how desperate and large inner city problems are, carefully selected grants could do some good, as they did during the era of the Front Porch alliance in Indianapolis.

Help Wanted

The Need for Presidential Leadership

The conventional press tendency has been to see "compassionate conservatism" as a feel-good phrase. In reality, the concept faces powerful and determined opposition. A river of suspicion divides America. Charitable choice and charitable choices threaten those liberals who do not want to relinquish power and those conservatives who do not want to relinquish cash. The Jefferson-Madison concept of benign separation, the Sumner-Newcomb doctrine of malign neglect, and the Lovejoy tradition in social work are among the historical barriers to any attempted advance.

For good reason, suspicion of Washington is high. If I'm looking for laugh lines in after-dinner speeches, I can always tell the story of a young farm girl who was out milking the family cow when a stranger approached and asked to see her mother. "Momma," the young lady called out, "there's a man here to see you." The mother looked out the kitchen window and replied, "Haven't I always told you not to talk to strangers? You come in this house right now." The girl protested: "But momma, this man says he is a United States senator." The wise mother replied, "In that case, bring the cow in with you."

Daniel responds to anti-Washington humor also, in his case because the only president he remembers is Bill Clinton—and that does not make him likely to trust national leaders. But something happened to him on our trip. At the end, he remained skeptical, but he would sometimes allow an exception. "Maybe once in a while that money can be used well," he said. "Seeing Pastor Herb Lusk in Philadelphia taking government funds, putting them to good use, and explaining his acceptance of them, was a real eye opener. And I'm impressed with how the Front Porch Alliance and Judge Payne in Indianapolis leveled the playing field."

The attitude toward city government of many leaders of faith-based organizations in Indianapolis changed during Steve Goldsmith's eight years as mayor. He worked with faith-based groups that were among the most committed to evangelism, and thus among the most unwilling to work with government agencies, fearing restrictions on religious and ponderous red tape. He worked to change the attitudes of government agencies that were suspicious of religion groups and viewed them as threats. He showed in one city what could happen nationally: if more religious leaders saw the potential and more governmental leaders were willing to lay aside suspicion and let faith-based organizations operate without impairment, great progress could be made.

Our citizens need to see and understand that a new and better arrangement is possible; such teaching needs to come from those with the authority to transform existing procedures so that the new arrangement can be born. We need to hear from a trustworthy source that faith-based organizations are part of the solution for America, not part of the problem. The one person fitting the bill is a president of the United States who is capable of conveying that understanding and doing nationally what Steve Goldsmith did locally.

Such a president will have to speak regularly about the importance of faith in God to poverty fighting and other social concerns. He will have to emphasize the positives of faith-based organizations and make it clear that they need the freedom to implement religious programs without being chained by the secular definition of social service provision. He will have to explain patiently that the aim is not to grant religious preferences, but to stop discrimination against social involvement by churches, synagogues, mosques, and other faith-based groups of all kinds.

Such a president will need to understand that those with messed-up lives can change. They should not be treated as either pets or worthless losers in the struggle for survival. Of all the candidates running at the end of 1999, George W. Bush clearly understands that best. When asked why some faith-based groups succeed where secular organizations fail, he praised programs that help to "change the person's heart. A person with a changed heart is less likely to be addicted to drugs and alcohol." He said he understands the nature of that change because "I've had some personal experience with this. As has been reported, I quit drinking. The main reason I quit was because I accepted Jesus Christ into my life in 1986."

Governor Bush has also been quick to say that people of any religion or no religion should be on a level playing field, and that it is improper of government to favor any variant of theist or atheist. Here again, compassionate conservatism may be shot at from different angles. Christians may not be amused when tax credits or government grants go to an Islamic organization that convinced alcoholics and addicts to straighten up and fly right in order to please Allah. Liberals will not be pleased if a fundamentalist group similarly benefits. Just as there is corruption in some governmental departments, some corruption will emerge in some compassionate conservative programs. But our society will have to live with that and work to contain it, because without freedom for religion, our inner cities have no hope.

The Need for Advocates

If tipping had been largely forgotten for decades, an announcement that the practice should be resumed would not work by itself. Or to use the more vivid metaphor offered by John DiIulio, if we meet a person who has been knifed and is bleeding, we cannot merely pull out the knife and pronounce him healed. Given the education in noninvolvement that many Americans have received—"the government is handling the problem"—it seems unrealistic to expect the new understanding of and by faith-based organizations to develop without some pushing and tugging.

Washington hands tend to obsess about laws: pass a bill, and the victory is won. But Great Society legislation by itself did little. The new welfare regime became dominant only when Lyndon Johnson's administration hired hordes of publicists and community action workers to communicate the sign-up-for-money message. Such exuberant outreach contrasts sharply with the silence following adoption of "charitable choice" in 1996. That quiet was predictable, since the concept had an ideological home in neither traditional liberalism nor much of conservatism, and potential beneficiaries were concerned about the possibility of religious corruption. The rest was silence.

Compassionate conservatism needs advocates as committed as those who marketed the War on Poverty three decades ago. Here's evidence of what happens without advocacy: Two years after its passage, the charitable choice provision was little used and little known. The National Congregations Study in 1998 found only 3 percent of a random sample of over twelve hundred congregations receiving government funds for social service programs. Only one-fourth of these congregations even knew of the existence of the charitable choice provision. Significantly, half of the religious groups that described themselves as liberal or moderate expressed interest in gaining governmental support, but only one-fourth of the self-described conservatives wanted to sign on.

The growth of compassionate conservatism requires more than passage of a law, because it requires passage over the river of suspicion. If it weren't for that suspicion, many of our leaders would not have forgotten that the Constitution and the American tradition promote religious liberty, so that faith-based options have to be given space even if a few among the public object. If it weren't for that suspicion, charitable choice would be seen as a civil rights measure, one that instructs government not to discriminate against religious organizations and to respect their character as religious organizations.

If the pattern of decades is to be reversed, we need on the national and state levels organizations akin to Indianapolis's Front Porch Alliance. Faith-based groups familiar with problems of the past will be willing to work with governmental bodies only if they see friends in high places. In Washington, creation of a faith-based advocacy office in the Executive Office of the President would help enormously. As a national clearinghouse for information on effective groups, an ombudsman for faith-based groups that need help in regard to any federal action, and as a spokesman for the concept, the new office would be enormously helpful. It might have its finest hours when disputes occur, as they are bound to. Take the rocklike faith of someone who believes that Christ changes lives, rub it against a rocklike state bureaucracy, and sparks will fly.

The advocates will also need to answer the criticism from right and left of plans for charitable choice and charitable choices. Those from libertarian perspectives need to see that if men were angels, pure voluntarism would suffice and governmental initiatives such as tax credits would be unnecessary. The threat of government interference needs to be acknowledged but not exaggerated. Daniel and I met bold and courageous people who were able to use government for helpful ends rather than be used by it for corrupt ends. Threats of entanglement do not signify that a new system could not work; they indicate that eternal vigilance will continue to be the price of liberty.

The left, meanwhile, will be looking for excuses to return to centralized control. On tax credits, for example, partisans of the old welfare state will look for and find examples of people using tax credits to bankroll charlatans. Those cases will make an impact on people who are startled to find that some among our fellow human beings are foolish, incompetent, or gullible. But advocates need to be ready to show that even with all the anticipated human error, a charitable sector in which the funds are allocated by individual private decisions will be less wasteful than the system that has ruled.

The Need for Discerning Journalists

Attacks will be magnified if reporters do not do their homework. The record is not good. *Compassionate conservatism* on election night 1998 was the phrase that launched a million computer chips, with articles about Governor Bush's statements abounding, but the analyses I saw were too simple by far. Many journalists seemed to equate all of conservatism with Social Darwinism. The press consensus has been that conservatives by definition have little or no interest in helping the poor, so anyone who does show interest must be a closet liberal or a clever hypocrite.

This misreading was not entirely the fault of the press. Many conservatives had not clearly defined their positions in the new, post-welfare-reform policy world. The meaning of *conservatism* in foreign policy was obvious when the task of checking (and eventually checkmating) the Soviet Union loomed large. Similarly, conservatives could be united in domestic welfare policy when the need to contain and eventually reduce the sway of the welfare empire was a common pursuit. But after the Berlin Wall fell in 1989 and welfare walls became smaller in 1996, conservatives became like the dog that caught up to the truck and had to figure out what to do next.

But here is a fault of the press: few political reporters have taken the time to see for themselves what compassionate conservatism is all about. The initial definition of *compassionate conservatism* as a glittering generality could be challenged seriously only by the reality brought home by a pavement-pounding trip. In none of the cities that Daniel and I visited were the leaders of poverty-fighting organizations satisfied with press coverage of their own groups in particular or poverty problems in general. They were tired of being either ignored or patronized, treated more as cute pet tricks than integral parts of realistic community revival plans.

Reporters who did spend time at faith-based organizations often made a different error: they tended to see churches and similar institutions as institutions or instruments to be measured by their effectiveness in delivering social services. And yet the primary concern of most churches, synagogues, and mosques is eternal destiny. In the course of helping to change deeper understandings, they also change lives here and now, but journalists (and government officials as well) need to remember first things. Reporters need to display sensitivity to long-term ends even as they examine effectiveness in changing the here and now. Covering compassionate conservatism in practice will be one of the hardest jobs reporters ever have, and one of the most important.

If some influential journalists choose to attack God rather than fight poverty, they will have the power to make compassionate conservatism a subject of ridicule or even revulsion. But as Dean Trulear, one of my guides to Philadelphia, put it, "Most young folks have never learned what it means to act heroically—yet if they're exposed to the possibilities, some people will be raised up to recover the ideal." The journalistic task is not to be an advocate for any particular organization. Faith-based organizations are not at all immune from corruption, and investigative reporters do great service by nailing thieves. But pervasive cynicism helps no one, including the cynic: journalists should be willing to call a hero a hero.

The Need for Specific Detail

Many conservatives have participated in an all-or-nothing approach. Since they see federal spending in many areas as illegitimate, they do not propose programs that would be better than the ones now in place, because those also would be illegitimate. The result is that conservatives win only when they cut the size of government, and few of those victories have occurred even during a time of Republican congressional majorities. Liberals win most of the time because they put their effort into developing liberal programs.

An all-or-something approach would be better: try to cut back on government, but when that does not happen, work to have improved programs. Going down that road is dangerous both because all-or-something distracts from a tax-cutting emphasis, and because conservative programs that are successful develop conservative constituencies, making further tax cutting more difficult. But I don't see the likelihood of huge downsizing in the current political climate, and in the meantime (politically, it is a very mean time) good programs limp along while some poor ones are pumped full of dollars. The best way to get a sense of this is to move from theoretical discussion to concrete detail. I'll do that in three problem areas: after-school programs, maternity homes, and crisis pregnancy centers.

Among after-school programs, a few like the Fishing School in Washington are receiving good publicity and doing well, but many others (like Hannah Hawkins's) are limping along. Many could be replicated but are not, and hundreds of thousands of at-risk children suffer. Meanwhile, large federal sources of funding for after-school activities, such as the 21st Century Community Learning Centers program, are closed to competitive bidding by faith-based programs. Maybe those federal programs should not exist, but they seem likely to continue at a time when no one wants to be criticized for taking candy from babies. They should be opened to competitive bidding from faith-based organizations of all kinds, including churches, synagogues, and mosques. These groups need to be encouraged to participate fully without having to change any of their essentials. The best way is to emphasize funding of after-school progams through vouchers that would allow parents to pay for activities of their choosing.

More maternity group homes are needed because each year recently over 300,000 unwed mothers under the age of twenty gave birth in the United States. Only about half of the mothers graduate from high school, and 80 percent have been hitting the welfare rolls. These teen moms used to be able to get apartments on their own, but the 1996 welfare reform law allows them to receive funds from TANF (Temporary Aid to Needy Families) only if they live in an adult-supervised setting. When that is not available because of abuse or abandonment by the parent or guardian, states have to provide or assist in locating alternative living arrangements. Since there aren't enough well-supervised group homes, many teenage mothers are placed in virtually independent living arrangements that can be hazardous to both frustrated mother and crying child. As long as Americans are paying large amounts in taxes for those programs, it's far better for funds to go for maternity group homes rather than the mothers. The mothers can then receive vouchers to be used at homes operated by the religious or nonreligious groups of their choice.

Compassionate conservatism can effectively help even individuals enmeshed in the most contentious issue in American society, abortion. Governor Bush in 1999 said, "America is not ready to overturn *Roe v. Wade* because America's hearts are not right. And so, in the meantime, instead of arguing over *Roe v. Wade,* what we ought to do is promote policies that reduce abortions." Bush took a lot of heat from some prolife leaders and politicians because of that comment, but it's accurate. It's a waste of time to go for all or nothing on abortion in our current political climate. Worse, it's a waste of unborn lives that could be saved. (One of my books, a history of abortion in America, shows that compassionate approaches have saved million of unborn lives over the past 150 years.)

A president can and should use his persuasive powers to help hearts become right. But several dozen crisis pregnancy centers have found that a specific piece of information at the point of decision making can make a big difference. The Dallas Pregnancy Resource Center reported in 1999 that "many women and their partners change their mind about aborting their child when they see their child's image on the sonogram screen." The Alternatives Pregnancy Center of Denver reported a typical case: a woman twelve weeks pregnant and leaning toward abortion "was under the impression that this baby didn't do anything." The woman "was just amazed" by the sonogram. When the father of the baby came in for the next visit, he also changed his mind.

Thoughtful people on the prochoice side also favor the use of ultrasound machines to produce these sonograms—pictures of the baby in the womb made possible by a technique like radar—because they want women to make informed choices. They know that those who react without knowledge often later feel cheated and abused. We don't yet have the statistics, but one reasonable estimate projected from experience so far is that one hundred clients a year at a crisis pregnancy center would make a different choice when they took into account ultrasound evidence. If one thousand centers had ultrasound machines, 100,000 more women could make an informed choice, and 100,000 unborn lives could be saved.

But that is a big if, because these crisis pregnancy centers are faith-based, volunteer-driven, low-budget nonprofits. Few can afford the $25,000 for an ultrasound machine and the cost of hiring a nurse manager/ultrasound technician and supporting equipment. And yet the federal budget for fiscal year 2000 has Washington spending $152 billion on health. Some $4 billion of that is under the authority of the Health Resources and Services Administration, which administers a wide variety of programs. One percent of HRSA's $4 billion amounts to $40 million. Again, my preference is for tax-credits or vouchers rather than direct grants, and state rather than federal action, but since the Supreme Court nationalized the abortion debate with its *Roe v. Wade* decision in 1973, and has kept state legislatures from greatly restricting abortion choice since then, federal grants to increase the likelihood of informed choice seem appropriate. My guess is that half of the crisis pregnancy centers would not apply for a government grant, if offered, for they fear government interference with their operations. But I suspect that the other half, if assured that government would not interfere with their counseling, would go for it; $40 million is enough to supply a thousand centers with ultrasound machines, with other funds allocated for administration, supplies, and so forth.

Dangerous? Yes, very dangerous. But for many of those committed to either informed choice or to life, the benefits will be worth the risk. In debating compassionate conservatism, we need to look at the principles, but the major breakthroughs come when citizens examine the specific detail.

The Need for Volunteers

Compassionate conservatism will need heroes to take root. It will need strong commitment from a president and from program developers and advocates who may lose votes and career mobility by sticking to the task. It will need serious, discerning coverage from journalists. They will need to compare the programs they see with others that currently exist, and not measure them against some abstract ideal.

Only then will the prospect for transforming change emerge—and only if the enthusiasm of civic leaders is met by a welling up of citizen willingness to show compassion. Daniel and I were most impressed during our travels by gritty inner-city residents who refused to give in. But tenacity will take the have-nots only so far. They need allies—volunteers from the world of the haves.

Daniel and I could see the need for volunteers not only in the abstract, but through the work of our own church in Austin, Redeemer Presbyterian. In 1997 the church began its New Start program, designed to help those on welfare make economic and religious transitions. I'm the elder at our church charged with overseeing the program, so I know that funding is not New Start's major problem. (The church has some affluent members who contribute generously.) Time is more often the opponent; many of our members, particularly those with young children, are hard pressed to get away from other duties at least once a week to make the one-to-one commitment that our program requires.

And yet every Tuesday evening, about thirty rich and poor people, plus their children, get together for dinner, Bible study, and mentoring concerning jobs, budgets, and life. At one dinner, client Lurah Scott explained that when she called Redeemer, "I was told that the church didn't offer one-time help. I came Tuesday night. I knew I needed more than one-time help, but I didn't want to admit that to anyone. I found caring people who were not controlling me; they were helping me, and not only with physical needs, but with spiritual grounding. I got nothing I asked for, but everything I hoped for." Kristen Davis, her partner from the church, said that she and Scott "had both been hurt by broken relationships. We had both struggled with sin and pride, so our meetings became times for friendship. People are never going to get that from a government office. I came in expecting to give, but I've received."

Happily, when we returned from our trip, Daniel decided to be a giver (and to receive as well). He volunteered to start up, under adult supervision, a tutoring program for the children of the welfare mothers and others whom the church helps. The tutoring part of New Start is called Smart Start, and Daniel, who has to be reminded repeatedly to load or unload the dishwasher, does not need reminders about his Tuesday night tutoring.

Daniel is not alone. We met in our travels people who were sacrificing much, sometimes for reasons they barely understood themselves. Don Williams is only one of the high-flying enterpreneurs in Dallas and elsewhere who are now volunteering big chunks of their time and money to push forward antipoverty efforts. Some of the businessmen are active for religious reasons, hoping to serve God. Others have hit forty years old and begun to ask the tombstone question: How do I want to be remembered? Earning more money in legitimate ways, of course, is socially beneficial, because success in a free market system comes from providing others with goods and services that they choose to buy. But those who want to help others in charitable ways can do great things if they apply to difficult questions the same tough-mindedness that they brought to their businesses.

Sometimes the desire to be of service cannot wait. One member of our church had cancer that was in remission for several years. Toward the end of 1999, it reappeared, and the situation was grievous. But he still showed up on Tuesday evenings, with his wife, to counsel (and provide with practical help like car maintenance) an inward-looking, terse, and tense single mom who week by week visibly softened. His daughter tutored the children. If his situation worsens, at least he will go out serving, and his wife and daughter will remember well those evenings together.

The Need to Move from Welfare Reform to Reformation

Compassionate conservatism is not primarily a campaign slogan. It evokes a debate that has gone on for at least two thousand years. Early on, Israel and Rome showed contrasting patterns of helping the poor. The biblical model emphasized gleaning, with direct alms going only to those who were truly helpless. Rome's welfare system emphasized bread and circuses: give the poor enough food to keep them in misery and gladiator contests to distract them from their plight.

Early Jews and Christians reformed welfare by emphasizing real change rather than governmental spare change. They believed in turning away from both idols and idleness: the able-bodied were to work. Some communities established the three-day rule, which meant that strangers received food and lodging for three days. After that, they had to go to work or at least show evidence of responsible behavior. If they sat around, aid was terminated. This was seen as compassionate, because all were created in God's image and capable in some way of helping themselves and others.

Over time, however, some began to see poverty as a road to holiness. They leaped from the biblical argument that the love of money is the root of all kinds of evil, to a belief that money and material things by themselves are evil. Some took vows of poverty and went begging from city to city, thinking this would draw them closer to God. Situations sometimes became extreme. A bishop in Lyon, France, five hundred years ago invited beggars from all over Europe to come to his city so parishioners could bolster their own efforts to gain, supposedly, salvation by contribution. Soon, local resources were overtaxed, and people were dying in the streets. Church leaders had to call the whole thing off.

It was time for a second welfare reformation. In Germany, Martin Luther criticized nonessential alms giving and emphasized the need for individuals and families to care for one another, with the church as backup. John Calvin in Geneva, Switzerland, taught from Genesis that poverty is not natural or desirable: "Men were created to employ themselves in some work, and not to lie down in inactivity and idleness." Reformation leaders did not believe it was compassionate to maintain people in poverty. Rather than thinking that poverty somehow led people toward virtue, they concluded the opposite. Calvin wrote that "when men are pressed by famine, they would sooner sell their lives a hundred times that they may save themselves from hunger, no matter what the price."

These leaders of the 1500s taught that the encouragement of businesses was a compassionate act and that all lawful vocations (including the equivalent of flipping burgers) were good. Deacons typically visited homes to verify needs, and churches provided help in emergencies. Over the long haul, leaders encouraged entrepreneurial thinking, and deacons sometimes used church funds to pay for tools and raw materials so that each individual or family had the opportunity to gain financial independence.

Work rather than begging, help to those unable to work, start-up help to those willing to work, but no help to the able but lazy: this was the compassionate conservatism of the Reformation, and it had an impact on Catholics and Protestants for several centuries. Now we've moved back to the ancient Roman emphasis on bread and circuses, and we need not only welfare reform but a third welfare reformation. This is not a cause for a single campaign or even a single decade. Compassionate conservatism is not a smarmy concept; it is a call to battle.

In this battle, advances and retreats alternate. Compassionate conservatism in Indianapolis during the 1990s had much going for it: a visionary mayor, advocates for faith-based approaches who knew how to get things done at city hall, a sympathetic newspaper editor, and some street-level heroes. Even so, with Mayor Goldsmith's retirement after eight years and his replacement by a Democratic mayor with different goals, the Front Porch Alliance is now having to reconstitute itself within a private foundation. Compassionate conservatism in Philadelphia during that same period had little going for it in terms of governmental or press support. Even so, small and large churches battle on, seizing opportunities but not holding them too tightly, persevering amid the ups and downs.

Politics is a roller-coaster, and leaders of faith-based organizations learn not to put their faith in princes. The faith-based groups that last, and the volunteers who persevere, are those who have faith in a God who lasts.

How Compassionate Conservatism Can Transform Your City: Books and Tools

S INCE CONGRESS passed welfare reform in 1996, new books on macro elements (national policy) and micro aspects (local initiatives) of fighting poverty have emerged regularly. Good ones from each year include:

- 1996 macro: D. Eric Schansberg, *Poor Policy: How Government Harms the Poor* (Westview/Harper-Collins).

- 1997 micro: Amy Sherman, *Restorers of Hope: Reaching the Poor in Your Community with Church-based Ministries That Work* (Crossway Books).

- 1998 macro: James L. Payne, *Overcoming Welfare: Expecting More from the Poor and from Ourselves* (Basic Books).

- 1999 micro: Deanna Carlson, *The Welfare of My Neighbor: Living Out Christ's Love for the Poor* (Family Research Council)

The Welfare of My Neighbor is particularly useful for those thinking of starting a faith-based organization because it contains lots of how-to information and many addresses and phone numbers of other organizations. A workbook accompanies it.

Websites also are multiplying, some more fruitful than others. For basic geographic and financial information about numerous nonprofit organizations, websites such as the AOL Foundation's helping.org are useful. But it's hard in most cities to gain discerning analysis as to which groups are effective. Houston is one of the few cities that is well served, and in easily accessible fashion. The Center for Renewal (www.centerforrenewal.com) began in Houston in 1997 with the goal of identifying, assessing, assisting, and replicating social entrepreneurial groups in the Houston area that are offering effective compassion.

The Center for Renewal and I have developed three sets of questions to use in assessing the work of antipoverty groups. The first set concerns the philosophy of the organization and is in ABCDEFG form:

1. Accountability. Does the program demand accountability of the people it serves? Are the people offering help held to standards of performance?

2. Bonding. Does the program foster one-to-one relationships between givers and recipients? Is mentoring an important part of the relationship?

3. Character. Does the program build character in the recipients? Does the program challenge recipients and helpers to stretch their self-perceived limits?

4. Discernment. Do the providers use judgment to give help on an individual basis that takes into account individual needs? Do they focus on giving a hand up rather than a handout?

5. Employment. Does the program require work by the able-bodied in return for assistance? Does the program empower those it serves to find and keep employment by imparting not only job skills but the life skills necessary to stay employed?

6. Freedom. Does the program teach recipients to live responsibly in conditions of freedom, or does it tend to maintain them in dependency?

7. God. Does the program foster true self-esteem by leading them to their creator and to the belief that each individual is made in God's image and thus has eternal value?

A second set of questions can be helpful in assessing the effectiveness of an organization that meets the first set of criteria:

1. Success rate. Does the program have a success rate that can be quantified? Have outside studies validated the results?

2. Cost per participant. Is the amount the group spends per person effective relative to the services offered and their outcome?

3. Volunteers. Does the group mobilize community strengths by effectively using volunteers? Does the program use the professional capabilities of those who volunteer? (A CEO ladling soup is wasted talent in a nonprofit that needs a business plan. Creative thinking can harness the professional experience of auto mechanics, electricians, computer programmers, accountants, and many others.)

4. Roots. Does the group have a circle of people within the community it serves who stand behind the work and vouch for its effectiveness? Did those who founded the program do it for pay, personal aggrandizement, or something else? Does the surrounding neighborhood support the program?

5. Replication. Has this program been replicated elsewhere, or could it be a model?

6. Financial accountability. Can the program offer proof of sound financial practices, with validation by an external source?

7. Future. Does the program connect people to religion institutions and long-term support groups so that new problems can be met?

A third set of questions is designed to elicit specific detail that may not have emerged in answers to the first two sets:

1. Could you show me your mission statement, current budget, and list of funding sources?

2. Could you tell me who your board members are and how active they are? Can the organization supply additional references?

3. Could you provide examples of success stories—situations in which the organization helped to change lives? If so, names, addresses, and phone numbers are helpful.

4. Could you give me a copy of your annual report and copies of any brochures or videos that you hand out?

5. Could I see your training manual for volunteers? Do you also have a step-by-step activity manual, or one about how this program could be replicated?

6. Could you give me copies of any press articles published on the program?

7. Do you have a website? If you do, please provide the address. How do you find it to be useful?

One more question needs to be asked, should an administration devoted to expanding charitable choice and charitable *choices* take office in January 2001. Here it is: Would you accept governmental help if you were guaranteed that, during the life of this administration, you would never have to give up any religious practices or theological distinctives? Today, a question of that sort seems to belong in a book of fairy tales. But perhaps in years to come, such a question will not seem so Grimm, and some answers will be joyful.

Governor George W. Bush's Explanation of Compassionate Conservatism

IN INDIANAPOLIS in July, Governor Bush concluded an attempt to define compassionate conservatism that he had inaugurated five months earlier by bringing together in Austin a group of scholars and policy analysts. Here is his speech.

THE DUTY OF HOPE*
Indianapolis, Indiana

July 22, 1999

It is a pleasure to be with you—among people transforming this city with good will and good works. The Front Porch

---

*"The Duty of Hope," July 22, 1999. Reprinted with permission from Bush for President, Inc. All rights reserved.

Alliance is the way things ought to be. People on the front lines of community renewal should work together. And government should take your side. Mayor Goldsmith, my thanks to you. You have set an example of innovative, compassionate government. And that example has become a model for the nation.

Everywhere I've gone in this campaign—from farms in Iowa to Latino communities in California—I've carried one message. Our country must be prosperous. But prosperity must have a purpose. The purpose of prosperity is to make sure the American dream touches every willing heart. The purpose of prosperity is to leave no one out—to leave no one behind.

We are a wealthy nation. But we must also be rich in ideals—rich in justice and compassion and family love and moral courage.

I am an economic conservative. I believe we should cut taxes to stimulate economic growth. Yet I know that economic growth is not the solution to every problem. A rising tide lifts many boats—but not all. Many prosper in a bull market—but not everyone. The invisible hand works many miracles. But it cannot touch the human heart.

The American Dream is so vivid—but too many feel: The dream is not meant for me. Children abandoned by fathers. Children captured by addiction and condemned to schools that do not teach and will not change. Young mothers without self-respect or education or the supporting love of a husband. These needs are found everywhere, in cities and suburbs and small towns. But the places where these problems are concentrated—from North Central Philadelphia to South Central

Los Angeles—have become the ruins of communities. Places where despair is the easy path, and hope the narrow gate.

For many people, this other society of addiction and abandonment and stolen childhood is a distant land, another world. But it is America. And these are not strangers, they are citizens, Americans, our brothers and sisters.

In their hopes, we find our duties. In their hardship, we must find our calling—to serve others, relying on the goodness of America and the boundless grace of God.

The reality here is simple. Often when a life is broken, it can only be rebuilt by another caring, concerned human being. Someone whose actions say, "I love you, I believe in you, I'm in your corner." This is compassion with a human face and a human voice. It is not an isolated act—it is a personal relationship. And it works. The mentors in Big Brothers/Big Sisters—spending only a few hours a week with a child—cut first-time drug use by 50 percent and violent behavior by a third. The success of this fine program proves the obvious: in solving the problems of our day, there is no substitute for unconditional love and personal contact.

I was struck by the story of a gang initiation in Michigan. A 15-year-old boy was forced to stand and take two minutes of vicious beating from other members without fighting back. At the end, he was required to stand up and embrace his attackers. When asked why he submitted to this torture, he answered, "I knew this was going to hurt really bad, but I felt that if I could take it for just a couple of minutes, I'd be surrounded by people who loved me."

Imagine a young life that empty, so desperately in need of real love. And multiply it by millions. This crisis of the spirit creates an expanding circle of responsibility. Individuals are responsible to love our neighbors as we want to be loved ourselves.

Parents must understand that being a good mom or dad becomes their highest goal in life.

Congregations and community groups must fight for children and neighborhoods, creating what Pope John Paul II calls, "a hospitable society, a welcoming culture."

A president has responsibilities as well. A president can speak without apology for the values that defeat violence and help overcome poverty. A president can speak for abstinence and accountability and the power of faith.

In the past, presidents have declared wars on poverty and promised to create a great society. But these grand gestures and honorable aims were frustrated. They have become a warning, not an example. We found that government can spend money, but it can't put hope in our hearts or a sense of purpose in our lives. This is done by churches and synagogues and mosques and charities that warm the cold of life. A quiet river of goodness and kindness that cuts through stone.

Real change in our culture comes from the bottom up, not the top down. It gathers the momentum of a million committed hearts.

So today I want to propose a different role for government. A fresh start. A bold new approach.

In every instance where my administration sees a responsibility to help people, we will look first to faith-based organizations, charities and community groups that have shown their ability to save and change lives.

We will make a determined attack on need, by promoting the compassionate acts of others. We will rally the armies of compassion in our communities to fight a very different war against poverty and hopelessness, a daily battle waged house to house and heart by heart.

This will not be the failed compassion of towering, distant bureaucracies. On the contrary, it will be government that serves those who are serving their neighbors. It will be government that directs help to the inspired and the effective. It will be government that both knows its limits and shows its heart. And it will be government truly by the people and for the people.

We will take this path, first and foremost, because private and religious groups are effective. Because they have clear advantages over government.

Sometimes the idea of compassion is dismissed as soft or sentimental. But those who believe this have not visited these programs. Compassion is not one of the easy virtues.

At InnerChange—a faith-based program run by Prison Fellowship inside a Texas prison—inmates are up at 5 A.M. and fill their days with work and study rather than soap operas. At Teen Challenge—a national drug treatment program—one official says, "We have a rule: If you don't work, you don't eat." This is demanding love—at times, a severe mercy. These institutions, at their best, treat people as moral individuals, with responsibilities and duties, not as wards or clients or dependents or numbers.

Self-control and character and goal-setting give direction and dignity to all our lives. We must renew these values to restore our country.

Many of these organizations share something else in common: A belief in the transforming power of faith. A belief that no one is finally a failure or a victim, because everyone is the child of a loving and merciful God—a God who counts our tears and lifts our head. The goal of these faith-based groups is not just to provide services, it is to change lives. And lives are changed. Addicts become examples. Reckless men become loving fathers. Prisoners become spiritual leaders—sometimes more mature and inspiring than many of us can ever hope to be.

In Texas, there is a young man named James Peterson, who'd embezzled his way into a prison term. But when he was offered parole, he turned it down, to finish the InnerChange course, which teaches inmates to rely on faith to transform their lives. As James put it, "There is nothing I want more than to be back in the outside world with my daughter Lucy, [but] I realized that this was an opportunity to become a living [witness] for my brothers [in prison] and to the world. I want to stay in prison to complete the transformation [God] has begun in me."

One example, but a miracle that is common. Sometimes our greatest need is *not* for more laws. It is for more conscience. Sometimes our greatest hope is *not* found in reform. It is found in redemption.

We should promote these private and faith-based efforts because they work. But we should also promote them because their challenges are often greater than their resources. Sometimes the armies of compassion are outnumbered and outflanked and outgunned. Visit Mission Arlington in Texas on a day they offer free dentistry, and people are often lined up at 3 or 4 in the morning. Or consider that only 3 percent of America's 13.6 million at-risk children now have mentors. These groups are widespread, but their scale, in some cases, is not sufficient.

It is not enough for conservatives like me to praise these efforts. It is not enough to call for volunteerism. Without more support and resources—both private and public—we are asking them to make bricks without straw.

So today I am announcing a series of proposals. And they are guided by some basic principles.

Resources should be devolved, not just to states, but to charities and neighborhood healers.

We will never ask an organization to compromise its core values and spiritual mission to get the help it needs.

We will keep a commitment to pluralism—not discriminating for or against Methodists or Mormons or Muslims, or good people of no faith at all.

We will ensure that participation in faith-based programs is truly voluntary—that there are secular alternatives.

And we will recognize there are some things the government *should* be doing—like Medicaid for poor children. Government cannot be replaced by charities—but it can welcome them as partners, not resent them as rivals.

Where do we start? Our nation is so prosperous that we can meet our current priorities and still take on new battles.

We will strengthen Social Security and Medicare. We will fortify the military. We will cut taxes in a way that creates high-paying jobs. Yet there is another priority. In my first year in office, we will dedicate about $8 billion—an amount equal to 10 percent of the non–Social Security surplus—to provide new tax incentives for giving, and to support charities and other private institutions that save and change lives. We will prove, in word and deed, that our prosperity has a purpose.

My administration will act in three broad areas:

First, we will encourage an outpouring of giving in America. Americans are generous with their time and money. But we can foster that generosity even further—creating fertile ground for the growth of charities.

Right now approximately 70 percent of all tax filers cannot claim the charitable tax deduction, because they do not itemize. We will give people who don't itemize the same treatment and incentive as people who do, rewarding and encouraging giving by everyone in our society, not just the wealthy.

We will provide for charity tax credits—credits which will allow individuals to give a part of what they owe in state taxes directly to private and religious institutions fighting poverty in their own communities. Individuals will choose who conducts this war on poverty—and their support won't be filtered through layers of government officials.

Second, we will involve the armies of compassion in some specific areas of need, to demonstrate how our new approach will work.

Here is an example. America has tripled its prison population in the last 15 years. That is a necessary and effective role of government—protecting our communities from predators. But it has left a problem—an estimated 1.3 million children who have one or both parents in prison. These are forgotten children—almost six times more likely to go to prison themselves—and they should not be punished for the sins of their fathers. It is not only appropriate, it is urgent, to give grants to ministries and mentoring programs targeting these children and their families for help and support. My administration will start bringing help and hope to these other, innocent victims of crime.

As well, we will encourage and expand the role of charities in after-school programs. Everyone agrees there is a problem in these empty, unsupervised hours after school. But those hours should not only be filled with sports and play, they should include lessons in responsibility and character. So we will invite the Boys and Girls Clubs, the YMCA and local churches and synagogues to be a central part of after-school programs.

We will encourage private and religious charities to be more involved in drug treatment and maternity group homes. We will bring programs like InnerChange to four federal prisons, to test if its early promise is fulfilled. And we will set up a compassion capital fund, to identify good ideas transforming neighborhoods and lives and provide seed money to support them—helping to expand the scale of effective programs.

Third, we will change the laws and regulations that hamper the cooperation of government and private institutions. In 1995, Texas officials tried to close down faith-based drug treatment programs because they didn't fit the regulations. When challenged that these programs were effective, one official responded, "We're not interested in results, we're interested in complying with the law." We solved that problem in Texas. If I am president, federal workers in every department of my administration will know that we value effectiveness above red tape and regulation.

We will allow private and religious groups to compete to provide services in every federal, state and local social program. We will promote alternative licensing procedures, so effective efforts won't be buried by regulation. And we will create an advocate position—reporting directly to the president—to ensure that charities are not secularized or slighted.

I visit churches and charities serving their neighbors nearly everywhere I go in this country. And nothing is more exciting or encouraging. Every day they prove that our worst problems are not hopeless or endless. Every day they perform miracles of renewal. Wherever we can, we must expand their role and reach, without changing them or corrupting them. It is the next, bold step of welfare reform.

To take that step, our nation must get beyond two narrow mind-sets. The first is that government provides the only *real* compassion. A belief that what is done by caring people through church and charity is secondary and marginal. Some Washington politicians call these efforts "crumbs of compassion." These aren't "crumbs" to people whose lives are changed, they are the hope of renewal and salvation. These are not the "crumbs of compassion," they are the bread of life. And they are the strength and soul of America.

There is another destructive mind-set: the idea that if government would only get out of our way, all our problems would be solved. An approach with no higher goal, no nobler purpose, than "leave us alone."

Yet this is not who we are as Americans. We have always found our better selves in sympathy and generosity—both in our lives and in our laws. Americans will never write the epitaph of idealism. It emerges from our nature as a people, with a vision of the common good beyond profit and loss. Our national character shines in our compassion.

We are a nation of rugged individuals. But we are also the country of the second chance—tied together by bonds of friendship and community and solidarity.

We are a nation of high purpose and restless reform—of child labor laws and emancipation and suffrage and civil rights.

We are a nation that defeated fascism, elevated millions of the elderly out of poverty and humbled an evil empire.

I know the reputation of our government has been tainted by scandal and cynicism. But the American government is not the enemy of the American people. At times it is wasteful and grasping. But we must correct it, not disdain it. Government must be carefully limited—but strong and active and respected within those bounds. It must act in the common good—and that good is not common until it is shared by those in need.

In this campaign, I bring a message to my own party. We must apply our conservative and free-market ideas to the job of helping real human beings—because any ideology, no matter how right in theory, is sterile and empty without that goal. There must be a kindness in our justice. There must be a mercy in our judgment. There must be a love behind our zeal.

This is where my campaign is headed. We will carry a message of hope and renewal to every community in this country. We will tell every American, "The dream is for you." Tell forgotten children in failed schools, "The dream is for you." Tell families, from the barrios of LA to the Rio Grande Valley: "*El sueno americano es para ti.*" Tell men and women in our decaying cities, "The dream is for you." Tell confused young people, starved of ideals, "The dream is for you."

As Americans, this is our creed and our calling. We stumble and splinter when we forget that goal. We unite and prosper when we remember it. No great calling is ever easy, and no work of man is ever perfect. But we can, in our imperfect way, rise now and again to the example of St. Francis—where there is hatred, sowing love; where there is darkness, shedding light; where there is despair, bringing hope.